Ken Sumrall and Church Foundational Network

Ken Sumrall and Church Foundational Network

A Modern-Day Apostolic Movement

Terry D. Shiver

WIPF & STOCK · Eugene, Oregon

KEN SUMRALL AND CHURCH FOUNDATIONAL NETWORK
A Modern-Day Apostolic Movement

Copyright © 2015 Terry D. Shiver. All rights reserved. Except for brief quotations in critical publications or reviews, no part of this book may be reproduced in any manner without prior written permission from the publisher. Write: Permissions. Wipf and Stock Publishers, 199 W. 8th Ave., Suite 3, Eugene, OR 97401.

Wipf & Stock
An Imprint of Wipf and Stock Publishers
199 W. 8th Ave., Suite 3
Eugene, OR 97401

www.wipfandstock.com

ISBN 13: 978-1-4982-2155-9

Manufactured in the U.S.A.   11/11/2015

Scripture quotations marked HCSB are taken from the Holmes Christian Standard Bible, Copyright 1999, 2000, 2002, 2003, 2009 by Holman Bible Publishers. Used by permission. HCSB is a federally registered trademark of Holman Bible Publishers.

All other scriptures taken from the New King James version. Copyright 1982 by Thomas Nelson. Used by permission. All rights reserved.

To my wife, Nancy

Contents

Acknowledgments | ix

1. Ken Sumrall and Church Foundational Network Cultural and Historical Antecedents for Modern-Day Apostolic Networks | 1
2. More Antecedents for Church Networks | 20
3. Ken Sumrall | 38
4. Liberty Fellowship of Churches and Ministers: Movement or Institution? | 52
5. Church Foundational Network | 72
6. Understanding the Modern-Day Apostle | 88
7. Concerns and Apprehensions | 104
8. Leadership and Directional Changes for Church Foundational Network | 121
9. Reflections | 140

Appendix | 153
Bibliography | 161

Acknowledgments

THERE ARE MANY EXCEPTIONAL individuals who deserve to be recognized. This monograph was drawn from my doctoral dissertation at Regent University, Virginia Beach, Virginia, and I want to thank first my dissertation committee chair, Dr. Vinson Synan, for his wise counsel and continuing support in completing my dissertation. To my other committee members, Dr. Eric Newberg and Dr. Dale Coulter, thanks for the advise in preparing for my defense and giving me much needed encouragement to finish. Special thanks to Dr. Graham Twelftree, who did not serve on my doctoral committee but continually encouraged me throughout my studies at Regent University.

To the staff, elders, and congregation of Christ Community Church in Lake City, Florida, I am very grateful. They were willing to give me time away for researching and writing. Thank you.

To my children and wife, what can I say? I realized they paid a great price with me in completing my education and this project. To my sweet Nancy, companion in marriage for over thirty-three years: you are a truly Proverbs 31 woman whose example of faithfulness is a model for all. I could not have finished without your support.

Lastly, I am grateful for my Savior and Lord, Jesus Christ. He met me at several critical points in this endeavor and guided me to finish this project. I am honored to belong to him and his kingdom.

1

Ken Sumrall and Church Foundational Network Cultural and Historical Antecedents for Modern-Day Apostolic Networks

Introduction

OVER A CENTURY AGO, Pentecostalism was virtually an unknown phenomenon. From this place of obscurity, Pentecostalism has grown into a vibrant form of Christianity that has transformed the church world in the United States and around the world. Particular to Pentecostal beliefs was the doctrine of the baptism in the Holy Spirit and their loud proclamation that the *charismata*, or gifts of the Spirit, are a present-day reality in the church. During the past two decades, another present-day reality that Charismatics have embraced is the apostolic reformation movement.

This New Apostolic Reformation (NAR) is a renewal movement that has grown significantly since the close of the twentieth century and has changed the shape of Protestant Christianity,[1] not just in the United States but around the world.[2] C. Peter Wagner, who coined the term New Apostolic Reformation, gave the following definition for the movement:

> The New Apostolic Reformation is an extraordinary work of God at the close of the twentieth century, which is, to a significant extent, changing the shape of Protestant Christianity around the world. For almost 500 years Christian churches have largely functioned within traditional denominational structures of one kind or another. Particularly in the 1990s, but with roots going back for

---

1. Wagner, "New Apostolic Reformation," 930.

2. For the development of the apostolic renewal movement in England see Kay, *Apostolic Networks in Britain*.

almost a century, new forms and operational procedures began to emerge in areas such as local church government, interchurch relationships, financing, evangelism, missions, prayer, leadership selection and training, the role of supernatural power, worship and other important aspects of church life. Some of these changes are being seen within denominations themselves, but for the most part they are taking the form of loosely structured apostolic networks. In virtually every region of the world, these new apostolic churches constitute the fastest growing segment of Christianity.[3]

This idea of apostolic restoration began to take root in the United States in the 1990s and came mainly from the nondenominational or the independent charismatic churches. This decade saw the expansion of existing churches through networking with other pastors and ministries. Wagner spoke of them as the "new apostolic churches." Some of their characteristics included charismatic leadership based on proven ministry skills and anointing, vision rather than heritage driven, contemporary worship styles, new prayer forms, outreach and mission orientation, and embracing a supernatural mindset. Wagner emphasized that these networks believe in the restoration of the fivefold ministries of Eph 4:11.[4]

These networks focus more on relationships, integrity, and cooperative diversity instead of a centralized hierarchy. The various networks endeavor to build personal relationships and trust between their respective leaderships, with recognition both of the apostolic authority of the network leaders and of the autonomy of the local congregation.[5] For example, one network's Order of Faith and Practice stated that (1) it was not a denomination but an association birthed out of Spirit-born relationships; (2) it would not own church property of those associate local churches; and (3) it would not violate the autonomy of each local congregation and would abide by the constitution and bylaws of each local church.[6]

These new apostolic networks were reported to be the cause for explosive church growth for the past several decades. Reports from China and Asia claimed that multiplied thousands were being converted each day. Latin America has also been experiencing significant growth. A report showed that there were about 275 million committed Christians in 1980.

---

3. Wagner, *Churchquake!*, 1–2.
4. Hockens, "Charismatic Movement," 503.
5. Iverson, "Ministers Fellowship International," 176–77.
6. Hockens, "Charismatic Movement," 504.

Cultural and Historical Antecedents

Since that time, data reflected that 80 thousand souls were coming to Christ each day, with 20 thousand of these centered in China.[7] When compared with the rapid spread of Christianity after Pentecost, these figures far exceed them. With these results, John Dawson declared that "it is now a season for the restored prominence of the ministry of apostles."[8] Examples of these networks include Antioch Churches and Ministries, Crusaders Ministers, Grace Presbytery, Dove Christian Fellowship, Harvest International Ministries, Morning Star Fellowship, and Grace Korean Church.[9]

This book will focus upon one network, namely Church Foundational Network (CFN), which was originally started by Ken Sumrall of Pensacola, Florida. It will disseminate CFN's history by linking it to its historical antecedents, probing Sumrall's charismatic beginnings and theological development regarding modern-day apostles, and examining the contributions of his successors. Additionally, it will argue for a non-cessationist position that these networks, and CFN in particular, posited concerning the office gifts of Eph 4:11–12, especially the ministry gifts of apostles and prophets. Moreover, it will contend for a renewal emphasis of the Spirit sending modern-day apostles to the church and world, which was a key conviction of Sumrall. Furthermore, it will document and concur that CFN has moved away from its charismatic origins and embraced a post-charismatic outlook. As such, it will outline and compare CFN and Sumrall's evolving position on the apostolic with others who have concerns with the apostolic movement itself. In the end, the progression of CFN's growth has revealed that routinization and institutionalization of the movement has begun. While CFN is presently committed to its apostolic paradigm of an organic governmental structure, several suggestions were made for it to recapture its momentum as a renewal movement.

Before discussing CFN, a look at the modern apostolic movement would be helpful. Its antecedents are essential to one's understanding of what follows.

---

7. Wagner, "New Equipment for the Final Thrust," 28.
8. Dawson, *Taking Our Cities for God*, 11.
9. Hockens, "Charismatic Movement," 507.

Antecedents for the Modern Apostolic Networks

Cultural Issues

Turning to America, historians and sociologists of religion widely posited a substantial restructuring among American religious institutions, especially after World War II.[10] Contrary to the "death of God"[11] predictions, the religious life of the United States remained quite healthy. But the market share of attendance in American churches has changed substantially. The mainline churches continue losing members. By the 1960s, church attendance had bottomed out at about 40 percent and remained that way into the 1990s. The largest losers were the liberal denominations. Many conservative groups made startling gains, especially Pentecostal and charismatic assemblies.[12] However, these trends were perplexing. Why would churches that teach tolerance, rationality, and scientific sophistication be declining while those that were morally strict, theologically intolerant, and demonstratively expressive in their worship be growing?[13]

The answer to this question is the values of the baby boomers. Boomers, individuals born between 1946 and 1964, don't like bureaucratic structure. First, boomers simply do not put as much value in loyalty to a religious tradition as their families did. Being raised a Baptist or Methodist does not determine their religious preferences. Second, they view tradition negatively. While they may have tolerated the classics hymns, they grew up on rock bands. Little wonder that they like churches with moving worship. Third, they value a personal religion instead of hierarchical, governmental structures.[14]

Examples of churches that adapted to the Boomers are Calvary Chapel, Vineyard Christian Fellowship, and Hope Chapel. Combined, these movements represented over one thousand churches; and as such, they have had a profound effect upon American Christianity. However, it is fair to state that these three Christian fellowships were just the beginning. The testimonies of these Protestant movements were the reason for the growth

---

10. See Wuthnow, *Restructuring of American Religion*.

11. Van Buren, *Secular Meaning of the Gospel*; Altizer, *Gospel of Christian Atheism*; and Rubenstein, *After Auschwitz*. These books support this theme.

12. Miller, *Reinventing American Protestantism*, 17.

13. Kelley, *Why Conservative Churches Are Growing*. Kelly treats these types of questions when discussing the decline of mainline denominations.

14. Miller, *Reinventing American Protestantism*, 17.

and proliferation of the independent churches. Over the years, thousands of these churches have been birthed, and many have formed associations through apostolic networks.[15]

Another reason for the growth of these new networks was the dissatisfaction with traditional denominations. Within their ecclesiastical structures, believers were faced with essentially two options for the foundation of their ministry. One was to trust people and the other was to trust those institutions people have created. Before the 1940s, the assumption was that institutions could be trusted—whether they were social, political, educational, or religious. This paradigm was culturally compatible with the religious environments of such bodies as the United Presbyterian Church, the Episcopal Church, the Roman Catholic Church, the Methodist Church, and other denominations.

However, with the rise of the civil rights movement of the 1950s, the assumption of trust in organized structures was called into question. Many more challenges were voiced by the generation of the 1940s and 1950s. The opposition to the Vietnam War, the disruption of the Democratic National Convention in 1968, and the rise in investigative reporting are just a few examples that showed the pendulum of trust was swinging.[16]

An example of this impoverished trust can be seen in the Protestant Reformation. It became clear to Martin Luther that the institution of the Roman Catholic Church was corrupt. At the heart of the issue was moral trust. Luther questioned the issuance of indulgences in which the pope would draw on the treasury of the saints to remit the temporal penalties for sin not only for the living but also for souls in purgatory. Luther decried his political distrust of the papacy when he learned that the money from the indulgences was used to aid in building the new St. Peter's which the pope was erecting in Rome. As a result, Luther posted his Ninety-Five Theses on the door of the Wittenberg Cathedral, which marked the beginning of the Protestant Reformation.[17] Luther, who began to distrust both old institutions and the people who staffed them, created a new structure that, it was hoped, would become the recipient of the people's trust.

There are several assumptions that one can make from these antecedents for the new apostolic churches. First, personal relationships would be the center for their congregations. They would know how to connect with

---

15. See Wagner, "New Apostolic Reformation."

16. Schaller, *Tattered Trust*, 44.

17. Latourette, *History of Christianity*, vol. 2, *Reformation to the Present*, 703–42.

each other. Second, a more productive investment of their time, energy, and creativity would be used to focus on identifying, reaching, serving, and assimilating their members. Third, laity would be equipped and released to implement the vision of their churches. Fourth, learning, unlearning, and relearning of individuals would occur better within a community of co-learning. Last, a new wineskin would be needed rather than trying to patch the old ones.[18] Ken Sumrall echoed these observations in speaking about apostolic networks. He states that there "is a need and a place for 'new wine bottles,' which are nothing more than newly established churches for this present-day move of God."[19]

Edward Irving and the Catholic Apostolic Church

Ken Sumrall founded CFN on the firm belief that God would pour out his Spirit upon the church like he did on the day of Pentecost, only in greater measure. Sumrall believed that the modern-day church would experience the greatest outpouring of the Holy Spirit in all church history. In doing so, God would bring a shift in the way the church would function. Sumrall saw this transformation culminating from several criteria. First, the Spirit was creating a hunger in his people for spiritual awakening. Second, the Holy Spirit was creating in the hearts of young Christians a desire for spiritual fathers. To accommodate the first two issues, God was raising up modern-day apostles and preparing the church to become an apostolic people. Last, God would be establishing a new church government from the Eph 4:11–12 pericope of apostles, prophets, evangelists, pastors, and teachers.[20]

In addition to the restoring of the apostle to the church, the gifts of the Spirit would operate in the church as well. If he were living today, Edward Irving would probably confess to a kindred spirit with Sumrall. Irving also believed that the Spirit was restoring the gift of the apostle as well as the charismata to the church.

Irving was born at Annan, Dumfries, in Scotland on August 4, 1792. He graduated from Edinburgh University at the age of thirteen in 1809 and entered into the ministry with the Church of Scotland. Irving passed his theological exams in 1815 and was licensed to preach by the presbytery of Kirkcaldy. In 1819 he became the assistant to Dr. Thomas Chalmers and

---

18. Schaller, *New Reformation*, 53.
19. Sumrall, *New Wine Bottles*, 12.
20. Sumrall, *Apostolic Fathers and Their Families*, iv–v.

worked with him for two years. In 1821 he received a call from Caledonian Chapel in Hatton Garden, London.[21] By 1822 he was ordained in the Annam Presbyterian and became the minister of a small congregation in London. By 1823 this chapel had become the center of attention of London's wealthy and fashionable society.[22] In short order, the church became too small to accommodate the group, and a new church was built in Regent Square. The impact of Irving was overwhelming—not just the content of his sermons but his presence and personality. Thomas Carlyle, who was Irving's lifelong friend, stated the following:

> To trample on the smallest mortal or be tyrannous . . . was never at any moment Irving's turn; no man that I have known had a sunnier type of character, or *so* little of hatred towards any man or thing. On the whole, *less* of rage in him than I ever saw combined with such a fund of courage and conviction. Noble Irving . . . generous, wise, beneficient [sic], all his dealings and discourses with me were.[23]

While Irving was gentle in his demeanor, he was passionate in his convictions. He firmly held to the imminent advent of Christ and rejected the popular evangelical view of his time that the whole world would be converted to Christ before the second coming. His views were strengthened when he translated Manuel Lacunza's book *The Coming of the Messiah in Glory and Majesty*.[24] He maintained Lacunza's main thesis that the second advent of Christ would precede the millennium and that the latter would separate the two resurrections. Namely, one would be a resurrection of the saints when Christ appears in glory, and the other would be the general resurrection and final judgment of the remainder of humanity. Moreover, Irving became equally convinced that the prophetic gift of the Holy Spirit would be poured out upon the church for a renewal of faith for the Protestant churches, which he viewed as having grown cold and worldly. For Irving, Lacunza's work brought the last days into an inspiring and refreshing perspective. It caused him to return to a largely forgotten hope of the

---

21. Flegg, *"Gathered Under Apostles,"* 46–47.
22. Margaret Oliphant, *The Life of Edward Irving*, 79.
23. Thomas Carlyle, *Reminiscences*, 230.
24. Manuel Lacunza [J.J. Ben-Ezra, pseud.], *The Coming of the Messiah in Glory and Majesty*, 57–59.

true church and provided for return to the urgency with which the early church preached the gospel.[25]

Irving's friendship with Samuel Taylor Coleridge also greatly influenced his theological development. In his early manhood, Coleridge held to Unitarian views through which he basically denied the deity of Christ. His use of alcohol and narcotics for relieving pain soon enslaved him and ruined his health, home, and career. In 1815 a London doctor took Coleridge into his home and through extreme accountability helped him to overcome his habit. He rejected much of evangelical faith, especially towards views of Scriptures. For Coleridge, the letter of the Scriptures was not as important as the spirit of the Scriptures.

When he came to London, Coleridge became mesmerized by Irving's oratorical skills. Coleridge would comment on Irving, stating, "I hold that Edward Irving possesses more of the spirit and purpose of the first Reformers, that he has more of the Head and Heart, the Life, the Unction, and the genial power of Martin Luther, than any man now alive."[26] As a result, Irving was highly flattered by Coleridge's attention and became deeply attached to him. Over time, Irving's thinking was affected by his friendship with him. First, Coleridge's Unitarian background caused his understanding of Christ's nature to be as something less than divine. Irving would enunciate a similar view. Second, Coleridge believed that the preacher, in delivering the gospel truth, was virtually the voice of the Holy Spirit.[27] The following diagram illustrates his point:

Christ=Prothesis

Holy Spirit=Mesothesis

Scripture=Thesis   Church=Antithesis

The Preacher

=Synthesis of

CHURCH AND SCRIPTURE

"the sensible voice of the Holy Spirit."[28]

---

25. Flegg, "Gathered Under Apostles," 328.
26. Coleridge, *Collected Works*, 10:143.
27. Dallimore, *Forerunner of the Charismatic Movement*, 61.
28. Drummond, *Edward Irving and His Circle*, 68.

Cultural and Historical Antecedents

This equation of the preacher being the voice of the Holy Spirit was especially bold. It was an example of the speculative opinion that would appeal to Irving and turn his thoughts toward the Holy Spirit. The seed for the restoration of the apostle was, thereby, seminally implanted. While understanding that humanity was heading for judgment, Irving gleaned from Coleridge the possibility of the transcendence of the spiritual over the material through the direct working of the Holy Spirit. By turning to Coleridge, Irving's thinking would be forever altered.[29]

Another influence on Irving was James H. Frere. Frere understood the French Revolution as the fulfillment of biblical prophecy. He rejected the gradual improvement of the world leading to the millennium. Society was still filled with uncertainty as Napoleon had died in 1821, which provided the background for Frere's thoughts. There was an ominous belief that either his son, Napoleon II, or his nephew, Napoleon III, would become a warlord as Napoleon had been. Many Christians of this time believed the world had reached the "end times." As such, the Antichrist would soon be revealed and the return of the Lord was at hand.[30]

Frere's book *Combined View* set forth rules for prophetic investigation. First, prophecies should be set out within a unity of plan. Second, images should have the same meaning throughout one's study of the end times. Third, visible symbols should represent visible objects. Last, the study of various words in the original language should be precise in one's interpretation.[31] Frere was able to press his premillennialist position at the Albury Conferences, a gathering of like-minded evangelical leaders. He was looking for someone who had the ear of the public so as to get his views out. He found such a man in Irving. In adopting Frere's views, Irving began to preach this new doctrine of the end times. Frere's influence on Irving can

---

29. Oliphant, *Life of Edward Irving*, 98. Irving's affection for Coleridge can be seen in the preface of his publication of his sermons from the London Missionary Society. "You have been more profitable to my faith in orthodox doctrine, to my spiritual understanding of the Word of God, and to my right conception of the Christian Church, than any or all men with whom I have entertained friendship. . . . your many conversations concerning the revelations of the Christian faith have been so profitable to me . . . and your high intelligence and great learning have at all times so kindly stooped to my ignorance and inexperience, that . . . with the gratitude of a disciple to a wise and generous teacher, of an anxious inquirer to a good man who hath helped him in the way of truth, I presume to offer you the first fruits of my mind since it received a new impulse towards truth and a new insight into its depths from listening to your discourse."

30. Dallimore, *Forerunner of the Charismatic Movement*, 72.

31. Frere, *Combined View of the Prophecies of Daniel, Esdras, and St. John*, v–vi.

be seen in the dedication of his book *Babylon and Infidelity Foredoomed*. In it Irving stated, "I had no rest in spirit until I offered myself as your pupil."[32]

Irving's belief in the nearness of the second coming of Christ, the restoration of the gifts of the apostles and prophets, and the restoring of the charismata evolved from the Albury Conferences, held in the private home of Henry Drummond. Drummond (1786–1860) was a Tory member of Parliament, a banker, and a very wealthy aristocrat. Tiring of his fashionable world of wealth, he turned his interest to religious issues, becoming interested in Swiss Calvinism. However, he soon devoted his time to eschatology. In 1819 he bought Albury house, which eventually became the spiritual and administrative center for the Catholic Apostolic Church that was formed by the Albury group in 1826. The purpose of the conferences was to examine the Scriptures, especially the prophetic writings, to ascertain which biblical prophecies had already been fulfilled and which were awaiting fulfillment in the future. Throughout their deliberations only the Scriptures would be used to support their conclusions. These positions from the conferences were published by Drummond in a book entitled *Dialogues on Prophecy*, of which Irving was a coeditor.[33]

In the eighteenth century, the postmillennial view was prominent among evangelicals. In harmony with the Lockean heritage of rationalism and optimism, evangelicals emphasized a continued success of the church, the improvement of humanity, and the culmination of history with the coming of a literal millennium. At the end of this age, Christ's coming was expected to set up his kingdom in a converted world.[34] However, the French Revolution had made the postmillennial view much less tenable. The conclusions from the Albury Conferences were in striking contrast. They surmised that the second coming of Jesus would occur before the inauguration of the thousand-year reign of Christ.[35] In 1825 Irving developed these ideas in sermons published as *Babylon and Infidelity Foredoomed by God* (1826), as well as a three-volume set entitled *Sermons, Lectures, and Occasional Discourses* (1828).[36]

---

32. Irving, *Babylon and Infidelity Foredoomed of God*, i.

33. Flegg, "Gathered Under Apostles," 34–41.

34. Sandeen, *Roots of Fundamentalism*, 5.

35. For a good summary of the Albury Conferences conclusions see Drummond, ed., *Dialogues on Prophecy*, 1:2–3.

36. Bundy, "Edward Irving," 803–4.

Cultural and Historical Antecedents

Irving came to believe that the apostolic charismata belonged to all ages and had been in cessation due to lack of faith. He was inclined to hold that the restoration of the gifts was aligned with the Second Advent. From Albury, their conclusions emphasized the preparations for the second coming rather than the event itself. *The Morning Watch*[37] reported that "if the period be not actually arrived, it is fast approaching when it will be necessary for the *Holy Ghost to make himself manifest* to God's children by visible signs, as it was in the first ages of Christianity."[38] An atmosphere was created for the charismata to reappear, which led James Haldane Stewart, who participated in the Albury Conferences, to publish a pamphlet calling for fervent prayer for the outpouring of the Holy Spirit. Only in answer to this prayer would the social ills of Great Britain be overcome. He referenced the scriptural promise of the partial giving of the Holy Spirit at Pentecost. The complete fulfillment was yet to come, and when it did the kingdom of God would be established.[39] The prayer was simple and included, "Lord, fill the earth with Thy power. Pour Thy Spirit upon all flesh. Convert the Jews. Convert the Gentiles. Destroy the power of Satan, and reign Thyself for ever and ever."[40]

Reports soon began coming in chronicling the supernatural occurrences in Scotland. First, reports began to circulate concerning Isabella Campbell. Isabella was sick of consumption and confined to her room. Upon mediating on the Scriptures and the nature of God, she became extremely sensitive to God's presence. She would pour forth ecstatic speech in her communion with God.[41]

Next, Margaret MacDonald and her two brothers, James and George, had ecstatic experiences. While being extremely sick, Margaret began to prophecy a baptism of the Spirit for her brothers. Coming home from work, she addressed them at length and finished by praying for James to be endowed with the Spirit of God. James calmly received the baptism of the Spirit. He in turn walked up to Margaret's bedside and quoted the

---

37. Published quarterly by James Nisbet of Berner Street, London and edited by John Tudor, who would later become an apostle in the Catholic Apostolic Church. The title was from Isaiah 21:11–12. The journal was published between 1829 and 1833.

38. *The Morning Watch*, 621, as quoted in Drummond, *Edward Irving and His Circle*, 135.

39. Stewart, *Importance of Special Prayer*, 26.

40. Ibid., 27–28.

41. Story, *Peace in Believing*, 294–301. Robert Story was Isabella's pastor, who chronicled her life's story.

Twentieth Psalm to her: "arise and stand upright." After repeating these words, James took Margaret by the hand and assisted her out of bed. Robert Norton, their pastor, reported this event in his book *Memoirs of James and George MacDonald, of Port Glasgow*.[42]

Equally remarkable was the healing and baptism in the Spirit of Mary Campbell. Mary, sister of Isabella Campbell, was sick with consumptive-like symptoms as well as a heart condition. James MacDonald wrote to her, commanding her to rise up into her healing. Upon reading James' letter, Mary was reportedly healed.[43] Shortly after this event, the MacDonald brothers began to speak in tongues. Many others followed. All were influenced by the preaching of John McLeod Campbell, who taught against the strict Calvinistic views of election. Alexander Scott, also, promoted them to believe in the permanence of the miraculous gifts of the Spirit.[44]

When the reports of the Campbells and MacDonalds of Scotland reached London, Irving made the gifts of the Spirit a major component of his messages. With the apparent healing of Elizabeth Fancourt, daughter of an Anglican clergyman in London, expectations of the miraculous were heightened.[45] Irving saw the miraculous healing of Fancourt as evidence that the restoration of the apostolic gifts was not to be limited to Scotland.

By the summer of 1831, manifestations of the Spirit began to occur. House prayer meetings met throughout London. A number of persons who attended Irving's church received the gift of tongues. A handful of this company attained a particular importance. These were Mrs. Thomas Cardale; her sister-in-law, Miss Emily Cardale; Miss Hall, governess in the family of Spencer Perceval; Mary Campbell; Edward Taplin; and Robert Baxter. They were known as the "gifted ones" and sat in a prominent pew during the church service.[46] With the exception of Mary Campbell, they were associated with professional occupations. However, Irving remained adamant at this time that such manifestations could not be allowed in the public services.

On Sunday, October 16, 1831, Miss Hall could not control herself and rushed into the vestry and prophesied. Even though she was behind closed

---

42. Norton, *Memoirs of James and George MacDonald*, as quoted in Flegg, "Gathered Under Apostles," 42–43.

43. Ibid., 43.

44. Flegg, "Gathered Under Apostles," 44.

45. Norton, *Restoration of Apostles and Prophets*, 44–45.

46. Dallimore, *Forerunner of the Charismatic Movement*, 132.

doors, the entire congregation heard her. The congregation became confused as many stood on their pews and others stood to their feet in order to understand what was happening. Irving tried to reassure the people with explanations from 1 Corinthians 14.[47] By the evening service, the church was packed. There was much disorder as Irving tried to preach on the gifts of the Spirit. Towards the end of Irving's sermon, Edward Taplin rose and gave a message in tongues, which he immediately interpreted: "Why will ye flee from the voice of God? The Lord is in the midst of you. Why will ye flee from His voice? Ye cannot flee from it in the day of judgment!"[48] Many screamed as they rushed towards the door. Irving prayed, "O Lord, still the tumult of the people!"[49] After he gained control of the meeting, Irving encouraged the people that what they had heard was the voice of God. By the following Sunday an immense crowd had gathered. As the manifestations of the Spirit began, there were calls of "blasphemy!" followed by hissing and hooting. It became evident to the supporters of both sides of the factions that the division was deep and a direct confrontation could not be avoided.

Because of the manifestations at his church, an appeal was made to the Presbytery of London on March 22, 1832. The hearing took place on April 26. The session asked Irving to abandon his teachings, which they regarded as not in the tradition of the Scottish Church. What troubled them was the active participation in the services by those who were not authorized ministers. Irving was censured for this violation and expelled from his pulpit. The judgment was published on May 2, and on May 4 the trustees of Regent Square Church locked Irving and his supporters out of the building. Irving and his congregation were forced to conduct their services in the open air. On October 19 they moved to the Newman Street Church for worship, which became the center of the Catholic Apostolic Church in London for twenty years.[50] Throughout these years, Irving came to believe that speaking in tongues was the "standing sign" for the baptism of the Spirit and the "root and stem" from which all other gifts flowed.[51]

Unfortunately, Irving's troubles did not stop with his reproof from the session. The months following, Irving's relationship with the presbytery

---

47. Pilkington, *Unknown Tongues Discovered to Be English*, 10.
48. Norton, *Memoirs of James and George Macdonald*, as quoted in Flegg, "Gathered Under Apostles," 52.
49. Oliphant, *Life of Edward Irving*, 324.
50. Flegg, "Gathered Under Apostles," 53–54.
51. Synan, *Holiness-Pentecostal Tradition*, 87.

continued to deteriorate. In March of 1827 Irving delivered a sermon in which he used the term "sinful flesh" to define the human nature of Jesus Christ. His sermon was made known to Rev. Henry Cole, who took it upon himself to investigate Irving's views on the incarnation. On October 18, 1827, Cole visited Regent Square to hear Irving preach. During Irving's sermon, he referred to the human nature of Christ as "that sinful substance." Cole published Irving's position that Jesus' victory consisted in overcoming the sin and corruption of his human nature. While maintaining that Jesus did not sin, he posited that the Lord's human nature was of a sinful substance, which he had to strive against and had conflict with during his life upon earth.[52] Irving had grounded his christological understanding on Acts 10:38. In enunciating his doctrine of the sinful humanity of Christ, there was explicit reference to the sanctifying work of the Holy Spirit in the body of Christ. His stress on the work of the Holy Spirit in the incarnation opened up his thoughts on the "sinful flesh" idea. Irving explained his position in his book *The Orthodox and Catholic Doctrine of Our Lord's Human Nature*. He gave a summary of the contents in the preface:

> The point at issue is simply this; whether Christ's flesh had the grace of sinlessness and incorruption from its proper nature, or from the indwelling of the Holy Ghost. I say the latter. I assert that in its proper nature it was as the flesh of his mother, but, by virtue of the Holy Ghost's quickening and inhabiting of it, it was preserved sinless and incorruptible. This work of the Holy Ghost, I further assert, was done in consequence of the son's humbling himself to be made flesh. The Son said, "I come:" The Father said, "I prepare thee a body to come in:" and the Holy Ghost prepared that body out of the Virgin's substance. And so, by the threefold acting of the Trinity, was the Christ constituted a Divine and a human nature, joined in personal union for ever [sic].[53]

Irving believed that his position reflected Article XXI of The Scots Confession of Faith and Doctrine of 1560. To not hold this position would make void the doctrines of the atonement, redemption, regeneration, and the work of the Holy Spirit. Furthermore, Irving did not desire to magnify the divine nature at the expense of the human, thus undermining not only

---

52. Cole, "Letter to the Rev. Edward Irving," as quoted in Strachan, *Pentecostal Theology of Edward Irving*, 27.

53. Irving, *Orthodox and Catholic Doctrine of Our Lord's Human Nature*, 53.

Cultural and Historical Antecedents

incarnational theology but also the true significance of the resurrection and its promise.[54]

What Irving added to the traditional themes of Christology was the Spirit's relation to the Son, especially in his eternal relation and in his temporal saving role. The Spirit brings a meaningful and assuring salvation to all. For Irving, the person of Christ cannot be separated from what he came to achieve. Irving's pneumatic emphasis in his christological views causes one to rethink the maxim, "the unassumed is the unhealed."[55]

The Presbytery of Anna did not agree with Irving's christological position. On March 13, 1833, Irving's status as a clergyman in the Church of Scotland was removed.

During the years 1832–1835, there was a gradual process of integration into an identifiable body of Christians. It would have been impossible for the various scattered groups to spread with a single communion without some form of centralized leadership. This circumstance provided for the emergence of an apostleship. Prophetic utterances called for apostles to be restored. Robert Baxter recorded such an admonishment in his book: "It was declared in utterance that the Lord would again send apostles, by the laying on of whose hands would follow the baptism of fire, which should subdue the flesh and burn out sin; and should give to the disciples of Christ the full freedom of the Holy Ghost, and full and final victory over the world."[56] On November 7, 1832, Henry Drummond gave the prophetic call that J. P. Cardale was to be the first new apostle for the Catholic Apostolic body. By December, Cardale had ordained Drummond and O. E. Taplin as apostles. By 1833 two more were added, and another two were in 1834. By 1835 there were insistent calls for the number to be brought up to twelve. Cardale and Taplin set out to visit the various congregations in order to discern who the remaining apostles would be. From their visits, the apostolic college was formed. It included John B. Cardale, Henry

---

54. Ibid., x–xi. "They argue for an identity of origin merely; we argue for an identity of life also. They argue for an inherent holiness; we argue for a holiness maintained by the Person of the Son, through the operation of the Holy Ghost. They say, that though his body was changed in the generation, he was still our fellow in all temptations and sympathies: we deny that it could be so; for change is change; and if his body was changed in the conception, it was not in its life as ours is. In one word, we present believers with a real life; a suffering, mortal flesh; a real death and a real resurrection of this flesh of ours: they present the life, death, and resurrection of a changed flesh: and so create a chasm between Him and us which no knowledge, nor even imagination, can overleap."

55. MacFarlane, "Christology of Edward Irving."

56. Baxter, *Narrative of Facts*, 65.

Drummond, Henry King-Church, Spencer Perceval, Nicolas Armstrong, Francis V. Woodhouse, Henry Dalton, John O. Tudor, Thomas Carlyle, Frank Sitwell, William Dow, and Duncan Mackenzie.[57]

Irving was relegated to a minor role in his congregation because he had received no charismata. Its members in London were divided into seven churches, of which Irving pastored at Newman Street. By 1834 Irving had developed consumption. He chose to visit Scotland, but despite prayer for healing, Irving died in Glasgow on December 8, 1834. His death occurred during the early formative years of the Catholic Apostolic Church. The eventual liturgical and ecclesiological advancements went far beyond what Irving had envisaged. It is a matter of speculation whether Irving would have approved of the ultimate outcome of the church.[58]

By the summer of 1835, there were seven principal congregations in London, each with its own "angel" (bishop). As such, they prophetically interpreted themselves as representative of the seven churches of Asia. Following Acts 13:1–4, they believed they were to separate some of the apostles for their work as ministers of the universal church. Also, a start was made to develop a liturgy that would eventually replace the various traditions of worship as the individual churches.[59]

By early 1836, Drummond called prophetically for a worldview understanding of their paradigm to adopt the whole world. Christendom was to be divided up amongst the apostles as princes of the tribes of Israel.[60] These apostles were commissioned to journey throughout the territories and assess the spiritual condition of the people.

In time, the movement's liturgical structure for the church surpassed the prophetic passion, and prophecy became less functional. It virtually ceased in the British church. As the apostles died out, Cardale expressed his disappointment that his apostolic colleagues had passed away and thus shattered the hope that the apostles would be alive at the Lord's coming to lead his people into their heavenly inheritance. In the summer of 1855, the remaining apostles concluded that no new apostles should be raised up so that the college could retain its full complement.

---

57. Flegg, "Gathered Under Apostles," 65–66. It should be noted that the social position of these men was either lower aristocracy or professional.

58. Ibid., 61–62.

59. Ibid., 68.

60. For the allocation of the tribes to the apostles see Davenport, *Albury Apostles*, 116.

Cultural and Historical Antecedents

However, in 1860 Heinrich Geyer prophetically called two angels to apostleship during a meeting in Albury. But the remaining apostolic college rejected Geyer's prophecy and instead decided to appoint them as apostolic coadjutors. The following year, Geyer, while visiting Germany with Woodhouse, called Rudolf Rosochacki to be an apostle. However, Geyer did this without Woodhouse's knowledge. This call was recognized by Friedrich Schwartz, an angel in Hamburg. The apostolic college, however, rejected his calling, and Schwartz and Rosochacki were both subsequently excommunicated in 1863. This schism was never healed.[61]

The German group continued at Hamburg by calling more apostles. It was known as the German Christian Apostolic Mission but later developed into the New Apostolic Church. It has more than 270 apostles, with more than 50 working today. Its congregations have grown, and they still claim continuity with the original Catholic Apostolic Church of England. In 1982 it published its most significant work, *New Acts of the Apostles*, which celebrated 150 years of the restored apostolate, the history of the Catholic Apostolic Church up to the schism, and the continuing history of the New Apostolic Church.[62]

In his day, Irving had been compared to many commanding personalities, including Martin Luther.[63] His ministry was one of systematic, doctrinal exposition of the Scriptures, especially his doctrine on the baptism of the Holy Spirit, whose "standing sign" was speaking in tongues.[64] His views also included the expected, immanent second coming of the Lord. With the manifestation of the gifts of the Spirit in his services, people were keenly aware that they were witnessing unique and novel events for their reformed church. Irving explained these charismatic expressions from Scripture, liking them to biblical Pentecost.

The beliefs and experiences of Irving and the Catholic Apostolic Church were very similar to the contemporary Pentecostal/charismatic churches. That there was no involvement between the two movements and that the last of the Catholic Apostolic apostles died a few months after the modern Pentecostal movement started[65] only underscores the power and

---

61. For an account of the details of the schism, see Woodhouse, *Hamburg Schism and the Apostle Woodhouse's Teaching*.

62. Internationaler Apostlebund, *Neue Apostelgeschichte* (*New Acts of the Apostles*).

63. Coleridge, *On the Constitution of the Church and State*, 154.

64. Synan, *Holiness-Pentecostal Tradition*, 87.

65. The last apostle of the Catholic Apostolic Church was Francis V. Woodhouse,

17

substance of the comparison. The theological development of Pentecostal thought added the idea that speaking in tongues was the "initial evidence of the Baptism in the Holy Spirit"[66]—an almost exact parallel to Irving's position of the "standing sign."

As the years passed, there emerged several streams of Pentecostalism. These included the Pentecostal Holiness movement, the Church of God in Christ, the Church of God, Oneness Pentecostalism, the Assemblies of God, the independent Charismatic Church, and several others.[67] These governmental structures included an episcopal form where authority resided in the bishop, a congregational type of structure, a Presbyterian government that emphasized the role of the elder, and the apostolic, which held to the fivefold ministry of Ephesians 4 as well as the gifts of the Spirit of 1 Corinthians 12.[68] In the modern-day apostolic movement, the number of apostles in the office and the function of the fivefold ministry was derived from the same scriptural interpretation and with the same authority as in the Catholic Apostolic Church. Hence, the modern apostolic movement owes much of its ecclesiological and theological development not only to Pentecostalism, but also to Edward Irving and the Catholic Apostolic Church.

Summary

In *The Hitchhiker's Guide to the Galaxy,* Douglas Adams told of people busily trying to figure out the meaning of the universe. After many years of work, a supercomputer spat out the long-awaited answer: forty-two. Of course, the next job was to figure out the question! Hence, it was one thing to have data and information but another altogether different to know what it meant.

This chapter has revealed some societal trends that have opened the door for change in the church world, especially concerning the meaning of the new apostolic movement. Discovering the significance of the new

---

who died on February 3, 1901. Agnes Ozman spoke in tongues on December 31, 1900, as a result of a spiritual quest based on a re-examination of Scripture. The similarities between Agnes Ozman and Mary Campbell were striking.

66. Dunn, *Baptism in the Holy Spirit,* 2.

67. For a good review of the various Pentecostal movements see Synan, *Century of the Holy Spirit.*

68. Gee, *Wind and Flame,* 93–149.

apostolic reformation seems to be revealed from history. The antecedents for the movement have given momentum over the decades and even centuries to bring a new direction for church structures. Ken Sumrall's Church Foundational Network embodied these governmental changes. However, for a clearer understanding, we will look at more antecedents that led to the founding of CFN.

2

More Antecedents for Church Networks

The Pentecostal/Holiness Connection

MOST OF THE HISTORIC Pentecostal denominations trace their origins to the Azusa Street Revival of 1906. History bears out that there has not been much dialogue with the fivefold ministry gifts of Eph 4:11. However, the New Order of the Latter Rain Movement became one of several catalysts for the charismatic movement of the 1960s and 1970s. This post–World War II awakening was characterized by reports of healings and other miraculous phenomena. It stressed the imminence of the premillennial return of Jesus Christ, which was to be preceded by an outpouring of God's Spirit. This was based in accordance with the former rain and the latter rain of Joel 2:28. It was understood as a dual prophecy of the Day of Pentecost as in Acts 2 and of the outpouring of the Holy Spirit that was to immediately precede the coming of the Lord.[1]

Churches that were birthed or influenced by the Latter Rain movement were usually independent assemblies with little or no centralized organization. This was an idea that Sumrall ready embraced as he developed the governmental structure for CFN. Some of the distinctive beliefs and practices of the Latter Rain movement that found their way into the charismatic renewal were the fivefold gifts of Eph 4:11, tabernacle teaching, the Feast of Tabernacles, and the foundational truths of Heb 6:1–2. While Sumrall's own research had led him to embrace the fivefold ministry of Ephesians 4, he received much encouragement when he attended

---

1. Riss, "Latter Rain Movement," 830. Also see Riss, *Latter Rain: The Latter Rain Movement of 1948* and *Survey of 20th-Century Revival Movements*.

a conference in Houston, Texas.[2] Sumrall, together with his close friend Charles Simpson, heard Glenn Ewing teach on the importance of the office gifts of Ephesians 4. Dad Ewing, as he was affectionately known, was the senior leader of Grace Gospel Church of Waco, Texas. The church was formed in 1948 as part of the Latter Rain movement.[3] There were several threads of comparison within the Latter Rain movement that connected it with the modern-day apostolic network movement, especially with Sumrall. Throughout its history, there were many who were stirred by the Spirit, especially those who were in dialogue with Ephesians 4.[4]

Historians have faithfully scripted the numerous individuals who were influential for the International Pentecostal Holiness Church (IPHC) and other Pentecostal churches.[5] As such, they have given opportunity for comparisons of those within the IPHC and thereby allowed for the connecting of the dots of certain individuals and the modern-day apostolic movement. One such individual was Benjamin H. Irwin.

Benjamin H. Irwin

Benjamin Harden Irwin was the founder of the Fire-Baptized Holiness Church. The IPHC was formed in 1911 via a merger between the Fire-Baptized Holiness Church and the Pentecostal Holiness Church of North Carolina. Both had traceable heritages from John Wesley and the American holiness movement of the post–Civil War era. Irwin embraced the holiness teaching of the Iowa Holiness Association and claimed he was sanctified. For him, this was a definite second experience following justification. But after reading John Fletcher's *Checks to Antinomianism*, he was convinced that there was an experience after justification and sanctification. This he called the baptism of "burning love," the "baptism of fire," or the "baptism with the Holy Ghost and with fire." He stated that this was a completely detached and subsequent experience to both salvation and sanctification.[6]

---

2. Simpson, email message to author, March 26, 2013.

3. Simpson, email message to author, March 27, 2013.

4. I am indebted to Beacham Jr.'s book, *Rediscovering the Role of Apostles and Prophets*, for its excellent bibliography, which has expanded my understanding of the fivefold ministry within the Latter Rain movement.

5. See Synan, *Oldtime Power* and *Century of the Holy Spirit*. Also see Campbell, *Pentecostal Holiness Church*.

6. Synan, *Century of the Holy Spirit*, 34.

There was an extremely emotional element to this experience with manifestations of shouting, dancing in the Spirit, and falling in the Spirit. Irwin taught that there were additional spiritual baptisms besides the baptism of fire. These included "dynamite," "lyddite," and "oxidite," due to the emotional and explosive nature from which their names can be inferred.[7]

By the end of 1895, the Iowa Holiness Association rejected Irwin and his message. Not to be deterred, Irwin and his followers formed their own organizations in Iowa known as the Fire-Baptized Holiness Associations, which soon spread to the southern United States. Many of those churches that turned to the Fire-Baptized movement spread throughout the region "like a tornado."[8] By mid-1898 there were Fire-Baptized Holiness Associations in eight states from Florida to Iowa. Each had its president and secretary to lead the association, while Irwin was known as the "apostolic father" over the whole movement.[9] While Sumrall never revealed any secondary source for his use of "apostolic fathers" in CFN, the similarity is uncanny.

This growth came to a rough stop in 1900 when Irwin confessed to "open and gross sin" and left the movement in disarray.[10] Many of the churches disappeared. The remnants of the movement were held together by Joseph H. King. King moved the headquarters from Anderson, South Carolina, to Royston, Georgia, in 1902. By 1907 King and most of the ministers of the church had received the baptism of the Holy Spirit with evidence by speaking in tongues. They had embraced the teaching of G. B. Cashwell, who had been to Azusa Street in 1906. In 1908 the church changed its doctrine to embrace the Pentecostal view on tongues, and thereby they became the first official Pentecostal denomination in the United States. In 1911 the Fire-Baptized Holiness Church merged with the Pentecostal Holiness Church and adopted its name for the new organization.[11]

There are several significant consequences from the Fire-Baptized Holiness history that have relevance for the charismatic movement and, especially, for CFN and the fivefold ministry paradigm. For example, Irwin's first publication of *Live Coals on the Fire* (October 6, 1899) featured

---

7. Ibid., 35.

8. Synan, *Oldtime Power*, 49.

9. Beacham, *Rediscovering the Role of Apostles and Prophets*, 21. Early in the movement, these associations were autocratic in their governmental structure, but shifted toward absolute control vested in Irwin.

10. Owens, *Speak to the Rock*, 40–41.

11. Synan, "Fire-Baptized Holiness Church," 640.

an educational enterprise known as School of the Prophets in Beniah, Tennessee. In 1899 Irwin was given seventy-five acres of land in Beniah and went on to build a headquarters and a "School of the Prophets" for the growing movement.[12] Many in the charismatic movement today have their own "school of the prophets."[13] Second, both the Fire-Baptized Holiness Church and the Pentecostal Holiness Church of North Carolina identified elders as part of the leadership of a local congregation.[14] Sumrall believed that the church should be apostolic in nature and governed by delegated authorities. These authorities were to be a plurality of elders.[15]

Joseph H. King and George F. Taylor

As has already been mentioned, King came in contact with B. H. Irwin's Fire-Baptized Holiness Association and received the third experience after sanctification called "the fire." He joined Irwin's group in 1897. When Irwin founded the national movement in 1898 in Anderson, South Carolina, King was one of the charter members. In 1900 Irwin asked King to assist in editing the denominational journal, *Live Coals of Fire*. Shortly after his arrival, Irwin left the church in disgrace after confessing to an "open and gross sin." King became the general overseer of the demoralized church. By the time of his death in 1946, King had led the denomination to include twenty-six thousand members in seven hundred churches in the United States. Also there were hundreds of churches on foreign mission fields.[16]

King's chief theological contribution was his 1911 book *From Passover to Pentecost*, which was an understanding for the Holiness-Pentecostal teachings of the early Pentecostals. Additionally, it was his introduction for G. F. Taylor's manuscript *The Spirit and the Bride*, written in 1907 and published in 1908, which had special significance for the modern-day apostolic movement. Vinson Synan called Taylor's book "the first book-length

---

12. Hunter, "Beniah at the Apostolic Crossroads."

13. See Hamon, *Apostles, Prophets, and the Coming Moves of God*; Cannistraci, *Apostles and the Emerging Apostolic Movement*; and Cartledge, *Apostolic Revolution* for how modern-day prophets function within the church.

14. See Crumpler, *Discipline of the Holiness Church*, section 2, article V; and *The Fire-Baptized Holiness Church*, article VIII,

15. Sumrall, *Practical Church Government*, 47; and *Apostolic Fathers and Their Families*, 106.

16. See King and King, *Yet Speaketh*. Also see Synan, "Joseph Hillery King," 822.

defense of the Pentecostal Movement in America following the Azusa Street meetings."[17] The introduction by King, who by this time was the overseer of the Fire-Baptized Holiness Church, provided an important hermeneutical principle not only for Pentecostal theology, but for the restoration movement of the fivefold ministry. He stated,

> Divine revelation was progressive in its unfoldment (sic), and the discovery of the meaning of the truth thus revealed is of necessity progressive in the understanding of enlightened Christendom. This progressive discovery of the meaning of truth, as we approach the ultimate completeness, implies limitation individually and dispensationally. No literature belonging to any particular epoch of the Christian Church bears the stamp of perfection.[18]

Notwithstanding, King was extremely committed to the revealed canon of Scripture and did not intend to add any other sources of canonical authority. He was advancing, however, that no particular view, whether it be the traditional holiness view of sanctification or the baptism of the Holy Spirit, had the absolute final statement regarding the intention and meaning of Scripture. His statement was a fresh invitation to look at Scripture with an open mind, with exegetical and theological soundness and in dialogue with the history of the church catholic as one reflects on its importance for the present and future. Many within the renewal movement for modern-day apostles and prophets have used this paradigm to argue for their restoration in the church.[19]

Moreover, in chapter 9 of Taylor's book, entitled "The Early and the Latter Rain," he hinted at apostolic ministry when he stated that the early rain was the period of "apostolic revivals" that followed the Day of Pentecost of Acts 2. He closed that chapter by stating that "God has the right to impart a new light to His children from time to time."[20] Taylor saw the progression of God's revelation in the church's rediscovery of justification by faith (Luther) and sanctification (Wesley). He stated, "We are coming back to God, to the theory of the Spirit dispensation. The Bible has been our chart for direction, but by the Spirit it is unfolding, returning to apostolic light."[21] But instead of connecting his thoughts with Eph 4:11f.,

---

17. Synan, *Oldtime Power*, 107.
18. Taylor, *Spirit and the Bride*, Introduction and 98–99.
19. See chapter 6 of this book.
20. Taylor, *Spirit and the Bride*, 92.
21. Ibid., 98–99.

he spent his time discussing the role of the Spirit in forming the bride of Christ in the context of a rapture-based eschatology.[22] Taylor's work was a "foreshadowing" for the fivefold ministry of today. In the end, he was unable to provide a historical connection from the first-century apostolic to the twenty-first century apostolic. Taylor spent his last years as a faculty member of Emmanuel College.[23]

Nickels J. Holmes

It seemed inevitable that criticism and controversy would develop from such a great move of God as the Azusa Street Revival. The Pentecostal-Holiness movement faced its greatest challenges from 1906 to 1920.[24] During this time of strife, many articles were written that primarily centered on unity of faith and doctrine. One such article had great significance and relevance for the modern-day apostolic movement. Nickels Holmes' article in *The Altamont Witness* discussed the need for apostles to be restored to the church. Entitled "God's Appointment," the article was first published on January 8, 1912, and republished on February 8, 1915. Commenting on 1 Cor 12:28, Holmes made the following comments concerning the need for the fivefold ministry gifts, especially apostles:

> Every one of these offices, which God hath set, placed, fixed—in the church ought to be of full effect and filled with men of God in faith and power. First, he set Apostles in the church. An Apostle is one sent out from the Lord with a message or mission. . . .
>
> The Apostleship is an office of the greatest importance and authority of all the offices conferred upon the church. When God set the Apostleship in the church he did not limit it to the life or generation of any man. We find nothing in the Bible that teaches that it was thus limited. The office is far greater and more durable than the person that fills it. The Apostleship was God's call to the man to bring him out to where God could put his power and authority

---

22. It should be noted that Taylor's views blends well with King's hermeneutic from the Introduction. Also, while Taylor's view of the work of the Holy Spirit is rather rigid, it is not paradigmatic for those who hold to the contemporary relevance of fivefold ministry.

23. See Synan, *Emmanuel College*.

24. Synan, *Holiness-Pentecostal Tradition*, "Criticism and Controversy," 143–66. This chapter gives a great description of the many challenges that faced the Holiness movement. Also see Jones, "Holiness Movement," 726–29.

> upon him. . . . The failure of man, lack of faith, and obedience, has caused the Apostleship to lose its power and authority. . . .
>
> So Apostleship, prophecy, miracles, and diversities of tongues should stand today with the same certainty and authority as teachers, pastors, evangelists, governments. . . . Let the church recognize it fully, and yield in perfect submission to God, receive the fullness of the Holy Ghost, according to the promise of the Father, and the results will be the same. Are we not substituting human means and devices for the power and demonstration of the spirit of God? God grant that the church may cry out for Pentecostal power, means and methods.[25]

This article is one of the most convincing references to the fivefold and apostolic ministry from the early IPHC historical documents. In fact, this quote of Holmes was sent to a couple of CFN leaders without revealing who the author was. Both thought that it was a quote that Sumrall had made.[26] As such, it contained several principles that were relevant and significant for Sumrall.

First, Sumrall and Holmes took very seriously the biblical authority of 1 Cor 12:28 and Eph 4:11f. These verses carried canonical weight both for the first-century church and the modern-day church. Second, Holmes understood that the fivefold ministers were to be officers in the church. He advanced a governmental dimension for the church. Sumrall believed that in the Ephesian 4 paradigm apostles were to function in the body of Christ to mature believers. Moreover, apostles were anointed to birth and establish governmental foundations for the church.[27] Third, both Sumrall and Holmes rejected any views that the gifts of the Holy Spirit ceased with the original apostles. Concerning the church being supernatural, Sumrall stated,

> Men were created to have fellowship with God who is Spirit; therefore they have a void in their life for the supernatural. If this void is not filled with the supernatural power of God, it will be filled by the evil one. Christianity was supernatural from its very first day, and it will be supernatural until the last. The Lord gave His church supernatural power to be witness of His resurrection, and the world will require no less in order to really believe it.[28]

---

25. Holmes, "God's Appointments," 3.

26. Lipscomb, email message to author, April 6, 2013; and Joiner, email message to author, April 5, 2013.

27. Sumrall, *Apostolic Fathers and Their Families*, 40–41.

28. Sumrall, *Confidence*, 59.

Fourth, Sumrall and Holmes embraced that apostles and prophets were as authoritative for the church and as essential as evangelists, pastors, and teachers.[29] Last, they understood the government of the church to be the operation of spiritual gifts, especially the office gifts of the fivefold ministers. If not, then the church would tend to exist for its organization. Without godly relationships, Sumrall maintained that the danger of any system of government was becoming legalistic, sectarian, and cruel.[30]

Summary

These leaders within the Pentecostal-Holiness movement offered incepted understanding for the modern-day apostolic movement. In fact, given more time and maturity, they could have been the watershed for an earlier beginning for the apostolic movement. In spite of these missed opportunities, their insights and beliefs enabled an open window for others to build upon their biblical paradigm.

The Shepherding Movement

The Shepherding Movement was an influential and controversial expression of the charismatic renewal. It emerged in 1974 as a distinct nondenominational movement as the result of charismatic Christians who were leaving their denominational churches and joining independent churches or prayer groups. While the charismatic movement had integrated diverse ecclesiastical perspectives under the apex of the baptism of the Holy Spirit, the Shepherding Movement was ecclesiocentric[31] because it sought to bring renewal to church structures, especially church government. The Shepherding Movement was ardent to discover new ways of "doing church" that would develop countercultural Christian communities.[32]

---

29. Sumrall, *Practical Church Government*, 48–53; *New Wine Bottles*, 127–39; *Apostolic Fathers and Their Families*, 37–57.

30. Sumrall, *New Wine Bottles*, 29–20.

31. See Clapp, *Peculiar People*. Clapp described need for renewal in the church's structure.

32. Simpson, telephone interview with author, March 9, 2012. While the movement has been called the "Shepherding Movement" or the "Discipleship/Shepherding Movement," Simpson, who is continuing the heritage of the movement, prefer the term "Covenant Movement."

Historical Summary

The movement grew out of the friendship between Don Basham, an ordained Disciple of Christ minister; Bernard (Bob) Mumford, originally ordained with the Assemblies of God; Derek Prince, a philosopher turned Pentecostal; Charles Simpson, a former Southern Baptist; and W. J. E. (Ern) Baxter, a Canadian Pentecostal. They were deeply concerned with the social malaise and institutional mistrust of many American Christians, which resulted in an isolated, defensive uncertainty about the future. Additionally, they saw the charismatic renewal as the Lord's response to these societal changes, and especially to the nominalism of mainline Protestant denominations and the Catholic Church. As such, the leaders were disturbed by the extreme individualism of charismatic believers and the lack of true discipleship. They were especially troubled by the lack of integrity and Christian character among charismatic leaders.[33]

Responding to their observations, the men committed themselves to mutual accountability and submission to encourage each other's personal and ministerial integrity. After their 1970 association, they continued to meet regularly, and from their mutual union developed their teachings on submission, spiritual authority, discipleship, pastoral care, covenant relationship, and Christian community. Their teaching materials grew through the use of books, audio tapes, and especially *New Wine Magazine*, which promoted their teaching themes. Particular to their growth were the many small groups and home meetings, which were led by untrained leaders. Also, the Jesus Movement had launched a vast number of young believers who were looking for leadership. The five men's teachings occurred during this leadership vacuum.[34] By 1975, thousands had responded and were networked together under their leadership. According to one account, the movement grew to one hundred thousand adherents and included as many as five hundred churches.[35]

In 1974 and 1975 a national network of churches and prayer groups were started, led by those submitted to the five. These churches in the network were nontraditionally structured and emphasized discipleship and pastoral care. They were led by lay "shepherds," who in turn were submitted to a lead pastor, who was submitted to one of the five principal leaders or

---

33. Moore, "Shepherding Movement," 252.
34. Moore, "Shepherding Movement," 1060–62.
35. Barrett, *World Christian Encyclopedia*, 722.

an appointed representative. The association of churches and pastors was always said to be based on relationships, not on formal organization. Their wide influence in the broader charismatic renewal movement gave rise to heated controversy over its teaching on authority and submission, as well as the emphasis on trans-local pastoral care. The controversy became public when Pat Robertson in 1975 denounced the Shepherd Movement through *The 700 Club*. Robertson charged that the five teachers were controlling the lives of their followers through overuse of spiritual authority. Other leaders would follow Robertson with their denouncements as well.[36] Controversy over their teachings would continue. It began to decline in scope and prominence from 1982. By 1983 Prince had quietly withdrawn, and by 1986 the remaining four men had dissolved their formal association and stopped publishing *New Wine Magazine*.[37] The leaders admitted to serious mistakes and some extremes in practices.[38]

The Shepherding Movement—Antecedent Analogies with CFN

The ecclesiology of both movements was driven by what the leaders understood to be a God-directed response to their times, and as a result it was not systematic. Their public ecclesiological teachings were a commentary on their actual developing practice with church structures. Both movements taught trans-local relationship concerning spiritual authority. All five leaders of the Shepherding Movement pastored other leaders in the United States and some internationally. This networking was not an ecclesiastical structure or a denomination. Rather, it was organic in nature because of its being based on relationship and, thereby, underscored one's spiritual authority. They taught that much of ecclesiastical authority was too external and excluded spiritual accountability.[39] For all five teachers, true biblical authority was relational and life-changing. Similarly, Ken Sumrall understood trans-local spiritual authority as influence that extended beyond the local church. For Sumrall, the New Testament churches were linked together by a higher level of administrators who ministered beyond the

---

36. Moore, "Shepherding Movement," 1060–62.

37. Ibid.

38. Buckingham, "End of the Discipleship Era," 46–51. This article covers Bob Mumford's apology for the errors of the Shepherding Movement.

39. McDonnell, "Seven Documents on the Discipleship Question," II, 117.

local church.[40] For example, Paul's letters revealed that he had apostolic oversight that extended beyond the local church. These trans-local leaders were from the fivefold ministry described in Eph 4:8–11.[41] Also, Sumrall taught that the church was a living organism based upon the New Testament pattern of community. For the church to function in power there must be a sense of mutual dependence.[42]

All five teachers of the Shepherding Movement taught the kingdom of God as a central motif. They taught that a new emphasis in restoration of God's kingdom would bring the believer into greater maturity. This maturity would be seen in the charismatic renewal growing beyond the spiritual gifts and the baptism of the Holy Spirit, where God would endow the believer with godly love and authority to impact the nations.[43] God's kingdom, his rule and reign in the earth, was expressed by spiritual authority. Hence by submitting to God's delegated authority, believers were submitting to the Lord. The church thereby would become the vehicle of this biblical ideal—the restoration of New Testament church order and practice.[44]

All five leaders developed their restorationist views from history. They taught that after Constantine the church lost its spiritual passion, which gave birth to dead institutionalism. But with Martin Luther's 95 Theses the Lord began his restoring work. They cited the English and North American awakenings as well as the Pentecostal and charismatic movements as part of this renewal continuity. They maintained that the fivefold office gifts of biblical government would help return the church to its primitive power and passion.[45]

Their restorationism caused them to be anti-institutional and to loathe any suggestion of becoming a denomination. Yet because of their growth they were forced to organize and develop doctrinal positions, which were characteristics of many church institutions. Ironically, many restorationist movements were blind to their own institutional and sociological existence.[46]

---

40. Sumrall, *New Wine Bottles*, 109–11. He quoted the following scriptures as supporting his position: Acts 8:14; 13:1–3; 14:23; 15:6, 23; 16:4; 1 Cor 4:15,21; 2 Cor 12:21; 10:13;13:10.

41. Ibid., 109–112.

42. Ibid., 27–30.

43. Moore, *Shepherding Movement*, 69.

44. See Hughes, ed., *American Quest for the Primitive Church*.

45. Moore, *Shepherding Movement*, 82–83.

46. Snyder, *Signs of the Spirit*, 273.

For example, while they sought to avoid any ecclesiastical structures or any centralized organization, there was a functional leadership structure that revealed a chain of command. They had centralizing doctrines and developed national and regional conferences. However, they never formally organized themselves into a legal corporation.[47] They maintained that the movement operated through a network of personal relationships.

Sumrall was also a firm believer that the charismatic movement was a restorationist movement that would produce lasting results. He was concerned to see God-ordained, Spirit-filled undershepherds feed and care for believers. Additionally, there was a need for "new wine skins" for the present-day renewal movement, especially in restoring God's glory to the church and to church government. For Sumrall, this restoration would include restoring apostolic fathers to the church. In fact, in the foreword of his book *New Wine Bottles*, Sumrall reprinted letters from individuals and couples who were crying out for spiritual fathers.[48]

The charismatic movement, for Sumrall, would result in the restoration of the early church's love, power, unity and joy. God's government, which was patterned after the theocracy of the Old Testament, was ruled through delegated authority. As such, David's tabernacle (see 1 Chronicles 15) was the greatest Old Testament type of the New Testament church. There was no veil in his tabernacle. The ark was available for all to see.[49]

To Sumrall, delegated authority worked best by restoring the apostle and apostolic government. He understood that the New Testament principles of apostolic government would restore the glory of God to the body of Christ.[50] Historically, Sumrall embraced the Shepherding Movement's position on restorationism, namely that from the time of Martin Luther until present there had been a gradual restoration of the glory of God to the church. However, Sumrall believed that the tendency of believers throughout church history had been one of imbalance. Churches had bounced from the wall of extreme individual freedom to an overemphasis on submission and authority. For Sumrall, too much stress on individual freedom bred anarchy, while strong teaching on governmental structure

---

47. It should be noted that CFN did form a non-profit corporation so as to legally ordain its ministers.

48. Sumrall, *New Wine Bottles*, 13–16.

49. Sumrall, *Practical Church Government*, 27–28. While Sumrall believed and taught that there was no veil in David's tabernacle, there is no place in scripture that explicitly states this.

50. Sumrall, *New Wine Bottles*, 40.

fostered sectarianism and too much dependency on human beings.[51] He posited that one's obedience to a leader must be unto the Lord. Submission was subordination to an office or person but did not require unquestioned obedience, especially if it went against biblical teaching.[52]

Sumrall, like the Shepherding Movement, saw the church being restored to the New Testament pattern. While the five teachers of the Shepherding Movement underscored the importance of the shepherd/pastor, Sumrall understood the restoration of modern-day apostles as key to the renewal. For Sumrall, apostles were spiritual fathers. The benefits for having a spiritual father (apostle) in one's life were important for anyone in the ministry. Sumrall outlined some very sobering statistics concerning the ministry. These stats included underperformance, low self-esteem, negative affect on family life, conflict issues with church members once a week, and no one to share issues with (i.e., no close friend).[53] Spiritual fathers would be commissioned to impart wisdom to the lives of his ministers, encourage and correct them, provide accountability, and, most importantly, build a relationship with them. Their primary responsibility was to motivate their disciples to become what God created them to be and fulfill their destiny.

Another antecedent position of the Shepherding Movement and CFN was their mutual commitment to covenant relationships. Simpson taught that God was a covenant-making and covenant-keeping God because of the death of Christ on the cross. Reconciliation established the believer in a relationship with God and with God's people.[54] For the Shepherding Movement, this theology of covenant was a major identifying motif. Believers were to commit themselves with the same type of sacrificial love and loyalty to their leaders and to other believers. When the apostle Paul spoke about "joints" in the body of Christ, Derek Prince interpreted Paul's words as "interpersonal relationships between believers whom God joins together. But what is the 'ligament' needed to keep each joint strong and secure? The answer, I believe, is: *covenant commitment.*"[55] The organic nature of authentic Christian community and constructive church government was best expressed through covenant relationships. The five teachers used the

---

51. Sumrall, *Practical Church Government*, 37–40.
52. Sumrall, *Apostolic Fathers and Their Families*, 32.
53. Ibid., 59.
54. Simpson, "Salt of the Covenant," 15–18.
55. Prince, *Discipleship, Shepherding, Commitment*, 46.

phrase "spiritual fatherhood" to accentuate the objective of spiritual authority through caring relationships.

Similarly, Sumrall taught that CFN was to reflect a pattern for church government that was "family." Like natural families, God's family has spiritual fathers who care for them.[56] At the 1995 yearly meeting of Liberty Fellowship of Ministers and Churches (LFMC), Sumrall proposed that the pattern for governing the church was family, and families were led by fathers. Sumrall had founded LFMC in 1975 with himself as the apostolic overseer. However, by 1995 he understood a weakness in the organizational structure of LFMC. He had made no provision for other apostles, who would be developed through the years to birth their own families of ministers. He stated, "Whatever we had done in Liberty Fellowship that God had blessed, I did not want to destroy. I just knew I had a call from the Lord to provide an arena where apostolic ministers among us could function as fathers of ministers who were related to them as their spiritual sons and daughters."[57] The relational aspect included more than just the minister. John Carney, a CFN apostolic father in Salem, Oregon, said that "there must be viable relations with the congregation to the point that they know that the apostolic leader knows and values their ministries, their spiritual DNA and the expressions which make them who they are as a fellowship."[58] The relationship factor reached not just to the ministerial level but to the entire congregation. For Sumrall, community equaled relationships.

Personal tithing was also redefined by the Shepherding Movement, and its teaching was accepted by CFN. The Shepherding Movement taught that tithes were to be given to one's shepherd personally. Within church practice, tithes were collected and given to the shepherd. These funds were then placed into a general fund for setting salaries for the shepherd based upon his productivity. The shepherd's needs were also considered in determining their salary. Church facility costs and other ministry needs were met by offerings beyond one's regular tithe.[59] Sumrall had a comparable view. Beginning with LFCM, Sumrall taught that LFCM ministers should tithe to the organization rather than to local churches. Sumrall interpreted Numbers 18 and Acts 4:34–35 as teaching that the tithe of each believer should be presented to those who are over them in the Lord for distribution.

---

56. Sumrall, *Apostolic Fathers and Their Families*, vi.
57. Ibid., 5.
58. Ibid., 9.
59. Prince, *Discipleship, Shepherding, Commitment*, 32–35.

For example, the early church received funds that were apportioned by the overseers according to needs. From this understanding, LFCM ministers were to tithe to a central fund used to support traveling representatives among the churches, supplement small church pastors' salaries, launch new works, or for administrative expenses accrued in oversight for the fellowship.[60] However, after the birth of CFN, Sumrall changed his perspective due to the change in his new ecclesiological paradigm of ministerial cell networks. Within CFN, tithing to one's apostle was "encouraged" but not mandatory.[61] Individual believers within the various CFN churches were to tithe to their church and not to their apostolic overseer.

An emphasis on male leadership is another similarity that CFN had with the Shepherding Movement. In the Shepherding Movement there was a strong conviction of the need for male leadership. As such, women were not to have governmental leadership in the church, and they emphasized the very different biblical roles for men and women. There was a strong conviction that men had relinquished their place in church leadership.[62] Sumrall was in agreement with these observations. While Sumrall acknowledged the amazing accomplishments of women throughout the history of the church, he did not teach that a woman should have authority over a man. He maintained that Gal 3:28 stated that women do not have the same authority as men in church government or in the home. He stated that the verse referred to a position of grace and not any place of authority. He did say that women could teach other women, minister with their husbands, and preach under the supervision of elders. Moreover, he held that Scripture taught that women should teach younger women, can be ordained as deaconesses and prophetesses, and can proclaim the gospel, but that they cannot hold any governmental office in the church.[63]

Perhaps the greatest antecedent that connected the Shepherding Movement and CFN was the mutual friendship between Simpson and Sumrall. Simpson met Sumrall at the Southern Baptist Seminary in New Orleans in 1960. Their first encounter reflected the passionate friendship that they enjoyed throughout their lives. Simpson was sitting towards the

---

60. Sumrall, *New Wine Bottles*, 117–18.

61. Joiner, interview with author, April 5, 2011. Joiner stated that each apostle has his own apostolic council. This council helps the apostle with pastoral/ministry issues with those who are submitted to him. However, it is the council that sets the apostle salary and allocates ministry expense for him.

62. Basham, "Leadership," 16.

63. Sumrall, *New Wine Bottles*, 147–50.

back of the room, while Sumrall was located in front of him. A friend of Sumrall pointed Simpson out to him and informed Sumrall that Simpson smoked cigars. Incensed, Sumrall approached Simpson and gave him a Christian admonishment that smoking is a sin.[64] If Simpson was to have an effective ministry, the cigars must go. Sumrall's comment to Simpson was short and to the point. He stated, "You should quit preaching or quit smoking!"[65] Simpson recalled his admiration for Sumrall's courage to confront him as the foundation for their friendship.[66]

From this first meeting, Simpson and Sumrall became close friends. They exchanged pulpits and had many other classes together. In 1964 Simpson heard Sumrall preach on the baptism of the Holy Spirit. At the time, Simpson was only partially filled. Three weeks later, Simpson received the fullness of the Spirit with the gifts of tongues.[67] By the year's end, Simpson was struggling to stay with the Southern Baptist Convention.[68]

Throughout the early years of the charismatic movement, both men spoke regularly at Full Gospel Business Men's Fellowship meetings. They made it part of their weekly schedule to spend time praying together over the various issues that each of them faced. Through this fellowship, Simpson began looking to Sumrall as his pastor.[69]

When Simpson was included with the other three teachers associated with *New Wine Magazine*, Sumrall was troubled. He questioned Simpson's decision concerning such a substantial commitment to them without serious consultation.[70] However, in the height of the controversy, Sumrall stood by Simpson. In fact, Simpson had asked the other three teachers to include Sumrall. But they didn't move on Simpson's request.[71] By 1975 the teaching of the Shepherding Movement began to circulate in Liberty Bible College and Liberty Church, which Sumrall was pastoring. One of Sumrall's associate pastors had embraced the Shepherding Movement, and the end result was that Liberty Church experienced a split. From this event, Sumrall developed concerns over the exclusiveness and extreme practices that he

---

64. Kelly, interview with author, May 12, 2012.
65. Simpson, email message to author, May 18, 2012.
66. Ibid.
67. Simpson, interview with author, March 9, 2012.
68. Simpson, *Challenge to Care*, 15–20.
69. Simpson, interview with author, March 9, 2012.
70. Moore, *Shepherding Movement*, 47–48.
71. Ibid., 158.

saw in the movement. By 1977, Sumrall openly renounced the movement, and he and Simpson experienced a painful separation. By 1978, Sumrall had joined Jim Jackson, Houston Miles, Jamie Buckingham, and others to form the ecumenical group National Leadership Conference as an alternative to the Shepherding group.[72]

However, in 1983 Simpson was reconciled to Sumrall at an Ideas Exchange meeting in Orlando, Florida. Sumrall stopped while addressing the meeting and apologized to Simpson. Later he privately served Communion to Simpson.[73] After they reconciled, they agreed to play golf regularly together. The golf course provided them ample time to discuss their ministries. Particularly, Sumrall would confer with Simpson about his concerns with the LFMC. In time the LFMC started to treat Sumrall as a figurehead, and its focus shifted to building the organization. Over time, Sumrall became increasingly frustrated with the direction of the LFMC. Simpson suggested that the organization needed a more "organic" approach to ministry. Both had a strong view of Eph 4:11, especially concerning the restoration of the modern-day apostle. They held that apostles were "spiritual fathers" and helped establish pastoral leaders and godly government.[74] Both of these leaders came to embrace a strong local church paradigm. They held that apostles have no authority in the local church, unless they are invited by the elders of that church to address an issue with them.[75] They proposed a decentralized structure of leadership for the various apostolic networks, which are based in relationships.

Simpson's relationship with Sumrall helped him to formulate his position on modern-day apostles. In fact, Sumrall developed his talking points for the first CFN meeting from one of Charles Simpson's teachings on vision.[76] Simpson always considered himself a part of CFN because of his relationship with Sumrall. Simpson's influence with CFN continued after Sumrall stepped down from leading the network. In 2009 he was asked to join the CFN national counsel. Simpson declined because he did not desire any criticism to be directed against CFN because of the issues of

---

72. Hocken, "Charismatic Movement," 487–88.
73. Simpson, "Interview: Older . . . Wiser," 69–70.
74. Simpson, interview with author, March 9, 2012.
75. Both understand that if they had planted the church in need of help, their authority would be more consequential than in ones they had not planted.
76. Sumrall, *Apostolic Fathers*, 9–14.

the Shepherding Movement.[77] From this time forward, Simpson remained supportive of CFN.

Summary

Oftentimes one can become so busy with one's place within organized religion that one is dulled to pressing ecclesiological realities. The modern-day apostolic movement has challenged us to dig deep into our own understanding of how the church should function. These antecedents have revealed the historical and cultural threads in the tapestry of the renewal movement in general and, specifically, in CFN. They revealed the need for a thorough reformulation of the way one envisions ministry and leadership—these two are inextricably linked together. For CFN, this natural link was discovered in the term "apostolic."

Ken Sumrall embraced this challenge and became an agent for ecclesiological change, especially for church governmental structure. As such, a closer look at his life will be beneficial for discovering the evolution of his views on apostolic church government. The next chapter looks at his personal history in the renewal movement.

---

77. Simpson, interview with author, March 9, 2012.

3

Ken Sumrall

Early Years

KEN SUMRALL WAS BORN in Ellisville, Mississippi, on December 24, 1926. One of eight children, his relationship with his father, Irving Sumrall, was stained most of his life due to his father's addiction to alcohol.[1] But his mother, Amber Bynum Sumrall Buchanan,[2] was the glue for the family and, as such, was a source of strength for him. Sumrall's mother made sure that Ken was in church. She sent him to Pine Grove Baptist Church, where he got a steady diet of hell-fire-and-damnation sermons. Because of these sermons, he was unsure of his salvation and was baptized three times in the Leaf River just outside of Ellisville.[3]

Ken, the oldest of the boys, was shouldered with much of the farm work due to his father's drinking problem. In time, he grew bitter toward all the hard work and responsibility and ran away from home at the age of fourteen. He finished high school living in the school dormitory and working for his room and board through a job at the local hosiery mill.[4] After high school, he was drafted by the army and was stationed in Austria shortly after Germany had surrendered in 1945. Consequently, he never saw any combat.[5] What he did see was a war-ravaged continent and a plethora of hollow-eyed, emptied, and displaced people. It was a sentiment that he deeply felt in his own soul.

1. Means, email message to author, February 8, 2012.
2. Means, email message to author, February 12, 2012. Amber divorced Irving due to his alcoholism. Later she met and married Gene Buchanan.
3. Sumrall, *From Glory to Glory*, 2.
4. Lamb, interview with author, February 21, 2012.
5. Sumrall, *From Glory to Glory*, 1.

Returning home, Sumrall's only reprieve for his emptiness of soul was his Harley-Davidson motorcycle. Most of his days, he would spend riding his motorcycle up and down the highways, back roads, or dirt roads. It seemed to be the only way to deaden his own soul to the emptiness of his own experience. Riding gave him the ability to sedate the uneasy feeling that he had brought back from Europe. While on the road, he was free.[6] But his answers were not in Ellisville.

Amber's intuition told her that her son needed a change. She informed Ken that her brother, Jack Bynum, had a well-paying job with United Gas in Pensacola, Florida, and she was sure that he could get him one as well.[7] He jumped at the opportunity. The change in scenery was just what he needed.

Jack and Mary Bynum welcomed Ken into their home. While there were no jobs at United Gas, Jack got him hired in the appliance department at Gulf Power Company.[8] Since the Bynums had no children, they treated him like their own son. In time, he found many motorcycle friends, especially with the sailors at the Pensacola Naval Air Station. He spent his free time on dirty tracks, cross-country events, and drinking with his newfound friends.[9]

The Bynums were devout Christians. Each night Ken saw his aunt and uncle reading their Bibles and praying together. He overheard their gratitude for bringing him into their lives.[10] Eventually, he would join them in prayer simply out of politeness. He knew his life was not right with God. But unknown to him, his selfish, care-free ways were about to be challenged.

After a day of riding his motorcycle, Ken came home looking forward to a good evening dinner. During their time over the meal, Mary invited him to attend church with them that evening. While this was not something he relished, he knew that his aunt and uncle had been extremely good to him, so he accepted their offer.[11]

That evening, Ken was introduced to Ed Hardin, pastor of Richards Memorial Methodist Church. The service was packed with people, and Pastor Hardin preached with fierceness. Ken became uncomfortable. However, his distress gave way to conviction. Pastor Hardin asked for a show of hands

---

6. Ibid., 2.
7. Ibid., 5.
8. Lamb, email message to author, February 12, 2012.
9. Sumrall, *From Glory to Glory*, 6.
10. Ibid., 6–7.
11. Lamb, email message to author, February 13, 2012.

from those who needed to accept Christ as their Lord and Savior. Ken responded but refused to go to the altar. The invitation song finally came to a close. He thought that he needed more time before making a public profession of faith. Within a few minutes after the close of the service, his aunt Mary was introducing him to Pastor Ed in the foyer of the church.[12]

Pastor Ed had seen Ken's original response to the altar call but was perplexed at his refusal in making a public confession. Understanding the seriousness of Ken's condition, Pastor Ed asked him straight out about the condition of his soul.[13] Ken was startled at his words and the boldness of his concern. In fact, he did not know how to respond. Not waiting on his reply, Pastor Ed invited him to a Sunday school room where they would not be interrupted. He followed, not knowing exactly why. Within minutes Pastor Ed was explaining to him from the Scriptures the reality of God's love and what Jesus Christ had done for him. For the first time, he understood the gospel and, above all, that Christ had died for him. That night he became a born-again Christian.[14]

Ken decided to make a clean cut with his past by selling his motorcycle. Next he was convicted about his smoking habit. He had been smoking since he was twelve, so putting down his cigarettes got him noticed at his job. His supervisor, Fred Baker, asked him why he quit. He told him about his experience with the Lord with Pastor Ed. With disgust and ridicule, Fred laughingly called out to the rest of his employees stating that Ken was going to become a preacher.[15] Little did he know that his caricature of him was prophetic.

Ken became a member of the Methodist Church. By the summer he was involved with the young people. During that time he met Wanda Ruth Till. Wanda was very active at the church, and she and Ken developed a close friendship.[16] Over time their friendship blossomed into love and marriage. On October 17, 1947, they were married with Pastor Ed officiating.[17] After their honeymoon, which was simply their little apartment on E Street in Pensacola, they poured themselves into the church. In fact, he would

---

12. Sumrall, *From Glory to Glory*, 9–10.
13. Ibid., 10.
14. Ibid., 11.
15. Ibid., 12.
16. Ibid., 13.
17. Means, email message to author, February 22, 2012.

later remember that the sum of their Christianity was attending church and tithing.[18]

After several months, Pastor Ed asked Ken if he would be willing to teach a Bible class. He was not really interested in Pastor Ed's offer because he had no interest in being that involved with the church. But within several weeks disaster would strike their lives. First, the electrical unions voted to strike against Gulf Power over their low salaries.[19] One day he found himself in the union hall during company time; consequently, the company fired him. Second, Wanda fainted the next week while riding a bus downtown. The doctor found out that she was anemic and pregnant.[20] The doctor strongly suggested that she quit her job for the baby's health. The next day, while they were on their way to Wanda parents' house, they were in a wreck involving three cars. At the hospital Wanda was examined only to find that the baby had died.[21]

Depressed and disgusted, Ken began to pray in earnest. During this time, he was introduced to a book entitled *Bud Robinson: Miracle of Grace*.[22] Robinson was a well-known Nazarene evangelist of the 1920s. Ken was seized by the fact that, while the Methodist Church had a solemn approach to Christianity, Robinson seemed to truly enjoy it.[23] He discovered that Robinson posited an encounter with the Spirit that he called "entire sanctification." Robinson referred to this experience as "the second blessing."[24] That night, he when to the church and asked the Spirit of God for the "second blessing." After several hours of prayer, he began to overflow with joy and ecstasy. He felt deeply cleansed and purified and the closeness of God's presence. For him, this experience was much deeper than his original salvation encounter.[25] While the problems of being unemployed were still a reality, he confessed a new certainty in his soul.

Soon Sumrall was offered a job selling insurance for Peninsular Life Insurance Company.[26] Within months his financial situation started to im-

---

18. Sumrall, *From Glory to Glory*, 14.
19. Ibid., 15.
20. Ibid.
21. Ibid., 16.
22 See Miller, *Bud Robinson*.
23. See Robinson, *Bud Robinson's Religion, Philosophy, and Fun*.
24. Robinson, *My Life's Story*, 51.
25. Sumrall, *From Glory to Glory*, 17.
26. Ibid., 18.

prove. Additionally, he was elected a steward at Richards Memorial Church. This position catapulted him into a deeper level of interest in sharing his understanding of the Lord's goodness. He began to witness to all type of people—including prospective customers—about God's love. He began having a notion that God desired him to preach. But, being a soft-spoken man, he simply did not understand how he could be a preacher. He decided to make a bold promise to the Lord. He proclaimed to the Lord that if he helped him to be the top agent in his insurance company for the year, then he would know that the Lord was calling him to the ministry.[27]

That was exactly what happened. By 1950, Ken was the number one agent in the North Florida area for the company.[28] He, however, had forgotten his promise that he had made to the Lord. Then one day, while speaking to Winifred Zoble, the church secretary for the church, about purchasing some insurance for her son, she interrupted him with a question that was totally off subject. She simply asked if he was going to ever start preaching. With prophetic precision she had shocked him into remembering his promise to the Lord. With great uncertainty about the future, he surrendered his life to the ministry.[29]

Ken informed Pastor Hardin about his decision, who was delighted with the news. Hardin arranged for him to speak on laymen's day at the nearby Ferry Pass Methodist Church. The sermon was only ten minutes in length, but over half the congregation responded to his altar call. From this service, he determined that the ministry vocation was his life's calling.[30]

Pastor Hardin then helped Sumrall to enroll in his alma mater, Bob Jones University. There he applied himself to his studies and was determined to make all As. Having been licensed in the Methodist church through Pastor Hardin's help, he was given a charge of a small, rundown mission church in the poor section of Greenville, South Carolina.[31] Patterning his preaching style after Pastor Hardin, his messages centered on "Hell's hot, heaven's good, and salvation's real."[32] However, many of his hearers were upset with his philosophy of ministry, particularly his preaching.

27. Ibid.
28. Ibid., 19.
29. Ibid., 20.
30. Ibid., 21.
31. Sumrall, *Practical Church Government*, 9–10.
32. Sumrall, *From Glory to Glory*, 24.

Within a couple of weeks, Ken was summoned to the district superintendent's office of the Methodist Church for that region of South Carolina to discuss his style of preaching and his message. Walt Smut, district superintendent, greeted him and began discussing why he called him to the office. The issue centered on his message. Smut admonished him to stop preaching about hell.[33] For Smut and the ministers in his district, Christianity was simply a good way of life. Sumrall began to list multiple scriptures concerning hell and heaven. Smut knew that they were at an impasse and decided it was best to pass this issue to the license committee to allow him the opportunity to explain his position.

While the meetings started with a sense of investigation, it soon became an inquiry of Sumrall's right to preach on heaven, hell, and the second coming of Jesus. The meeting droned on until Sumrall became angry. He pulled out a copy of the Methodist handbook and placed it on the table. All eyes turned to Sumrall. From the manual, he quoted that John Wesley stated that anyone who wanted to join the Methodist Society must first flee the wrath to come.[34] He accused the group of ministers of not being concerned for the flock of God or for their eternal destiny. With these comments from him, the meeting erupted into a heated debate.[35] In the end, he resigned from the Methodist Church and turned in his license to minister.

Baptist Heritage

After this Sumrall asked several ministerial students to pray with him for direction for his life. The next day he drove around Greenville looking for the answer to his prayers for direction. He stopped at the cotton mill section of Greenville, known as Old Bleachery Road, a poor section of town. He noticed that there were no churches in the area. Walking down the road, he saw a building that was empty and needing repair. After securing permission from the owner, he approached his brother-in-law, James Vanderford, asking for help in repairing the building and in assisting with birthing a new church.[36] Vanderford had several Baptist preachers who he thought would donate to the new church. Within a few days, ten wooden benches and fifty worn out, backless Broadman hymnals arrived. Sumrall bought a

---

33. Ibid., 24–25.
34. Ibid., 26.
35. Sumrall, *Practical Church Government*, 9–10.
36. Sumrall, *From Glory to Glory*, 32.

piano for five dollars down and five dollars a month. In late November of 1951, the People's Gospel Mission had its first service.[37]

As months passed, word got out about the new church. Kids, old woman, and a few men started attending and receiving salvation. Because of Sumrall's fiery, passionate sermons, the building was soon filled, and they needed more room. Clarence Goodnough, a building contractor, volunteered to help with the building of a new church.[38] The people, who were mostly under paid mill workers, responded with their labor. Through their efforts they completed their new building, which was built up the road from the People's Gospel Mission. Sumrall named the new facility Hilltop Baptist Church.[39]

Hell was Sumrall's choice subject. Additionally, he had a hard concept of God. Because of this supposition, he would have a perception that God was never really satisfied with his ministry.[40] This performance mentality would surface again and again in his future ministry.

During the next three years, Sumrall would see people leave the church due to his fiery messages, while others were attracted to the church because of his fervent evangelistic preaching. Overall the church continued to grow. However, he would ponder over the logistics of church machinery, especially church government. Was his church typical of other churches? It seemed that he was doing most of the ministry work for the growth of the church.[41]

With Hilltop Baptist growing, Sumrall decided to accept a call to a larger congregation. In 1954 he became the senior pastor of Airport Baptist Church in Greenville. The people at Airport were of a different social class, and he felt a strong pressure to be successful. Anytime he missed a Sunday goal, he would be depressed for days.[42] Something was missing in his life and ministry. But he was unsure if it was the congregation, the way a Baptist church functioned, his bivocational status, or the pressure of being in school full-time. In time the pressure of performing began to affect his health. He began having excruciating pain in his chest, back, and under his

---

37. Ibid., 33.
38. Ibid.
39. Sumrall, *Practical Church Government*, 10–11.
40. Sumrall, *From Glory to Glory*, 34.
41. At this early stage in his ministry, Sumrall began pondering on the concept of team ministry and the importance of relationships for the ministry to advance.
42 Sumrall, *From Glory to Glory*, 35.

left ribs. The church leadership sent him to a hospital in Winston-Salem, North Carolina.[43] After numerous tests, the doctors attributed his physical condition to stress. He decided to make a clean break from these pressures in his life. He resigned from Airport Baptist Church, quit Bob Jones University, quit his part-time job at Western Auto, and drove back to Mississippi to visit relatives around Ellisville.[44] During this break, he began to ponder the importance for church leaders to create godly relationships to help them in their ministry. These thoughts would surface again in his future.

While visiting his family, Sumrall drove to Hattiesburg, Mississippi, to visit William Carey College. The campus was very appealing to both Ken and Wanda. He applied for admission and matriculated into William Carey during the fall semester of 1955.[45]

Wanda and Ken moved into a drafty two-story house at 600 Tuscan Street in Hattiesburg.[46] Ken visited that local Western Auto store looking for a sales position and was hired immediately. The manager, Harley Spinks, introduced him to Q. C. Barrett, who was the pastor of Green's Creek Baptist Church. Upon hearing that Ken was a preacher, he invited him to fill his pulpit the following Sunday. He was very reluctant, but Barrett prevailed with his insistence until he finally agreed.[47] The people responded favorable to his style and message, so Barrett invited him back several more times. During one of his messages, a pulpit committee from New Hope Baptist Church heard him preach. They immediately issued him a call to be their pastor. While he asked for more time to consider his decision, he ultimately accepted the position in December 1955.[48]

For over two years the church grew under Sumrall's fiery, passionate style of preaching. But by the third year he started having problems with his deacon board. At issue was his strong devotion to be the visionary for the church. In order to have more freedom to lead, he initiated a rotation system for the service time of the deacons.[49] Moreover, he began having some of the same health problems he had experienced in South Carolina. If he missed a goal, he would be depressed for days. After days of reflection, he concluded

43. Ibid., 36.
44. Ibid., 38.
45. Ibid., 41.
46. Ibid.
47. Ibid., 42.
48. Ibid., 43.
49. Ibid., 44.

that he was missing the power of God in his life. By December 1958 he had become so completely restless that he resigned from New Hope.[50]

Sumrall then started a traveling ministry as an evangelist, as well as a Sundaymorning radio program called "Christ for the South." But the travel put too much stress on his family life, and he soon accepted a call to the First Baptist Church of Clara, Mississippi.[51] This church was one of his greatest challenges. While at New Hope, he finished two degrees—a bachelor's degree from William Carey College and a master's degree from University of Southern Mississippi. All his educational success and his blazing sermons on hell did not seem to ignite the lethargic congregation at First Baptist. In the end, he felt like a hireling. In disgust, he tried to resign as pastor. He had told the deacon board that he desired to continue his education at New Orleans Baptist Theological Seminary.[52] They talked him into staying and preaching on Sunday. But they also gave him the time he needed to attend school. During his four-hour drive to New Orleans, he would wonder about his life as a minister. Among his concerns was why church governments seemed so rigid and inflexible. Why did denominations tend to be too ceremonial in nature? Why did church boards hire and fire ministers according to the whims of the congregation? And perhaps most important, was the church operating without really experiencing the power of God?[53]

Sumrall graduated from seminary in the fall semester of 1961. Three months prior, he had accepted a call to Boulevard Baptist Church in Pensacola, Florida.[54] This was his first opportunity to lead a thriving church in a large city. Even though the church had its problems, he remained faithful. By early 1963, the growth of the church pushed it into constructing a new sanctuary.[55] After the adventure of building the new facility had been realized, he noticed a lack of commitment among the people. Soon attendance started to drop, and the deacon board was wondering if they need to call for a "vote of confidence" concerning his leadership. He faced the opposition by recalling his studies in seminary. He had studied the lives of John Wesley, George Whitefield, Charles Finney, and D. L. Moody. In all their

50. Ibid., 48.
51. Ibid., 49.
52. Ibid., 50–51.
53. Sumrall, *Practical Church Government*, 11–12.
54. Sumrall, *From Glory to Glory*, 53.
55. Ibid., 57.

ministries, prayer was a key component.⁵⁶ He suggested what they needed was an outpouring of the Holy Spirit much like these heroes of the faith had experience. His board agreed, and they started a Saturday night prayer meeting called "The Hour of Power."⁵⁷ Sumrall was about to get some answers to his concerns for the ministry and his personal life.

Baptism of the Holy Spirit

The answer to their Saturday night prayer meetings came through a young woman, June Gordon. June was the director of the church's youth "Sunbeam" program. Asking for a meeting with Sumrall, she informed him that she had been baptized in the Holy Spirit and had spoken in tongues. June was a sensible person and not given to emotional extremes. So when he asked her not to use her new gift, he was sure she would honor his request. She did obey his petition, but began sharing her experience privately with her friends. Before long, the Women's Missionary Union (WMU) president, a deacon and his wife, and a young minister had all received the experience.⁵⁸

Sumrall chose not to denounce the experience from the pulpit, but did teach that the tongues gift was the least of the gifts and caused too much trouble to be desired. Eventually, he became more outspoken, and as a result some of the church's faithful left to attend Pentecostal churches in the area. He had been taught a cessationist position throughout his education. Miracles were used to establish the church until the Bible was written and canonized, then they ceased.⁵⁹ However, he became perplexed after reading an article by Billy Graham in *Voice Magazine*. In the article, Graham did not endorse any gifts of the Spirit but expressed his confidence that the Spirit of the Lord was moving in a fresh way in the United States. Graham stated that he believed this new movement was from God.⁶⁰ The article got Sumrall's attention.⁶¹

Sumrall decided to call Graham's office and ask them to send someone to his church for an evangelical outreach. When they came, he met Joe

56. Ibid., 59.
57. Ibid., 59.
58. Ibid., 61–62.
59. Ibid., 63.
60 Graham, "I Thank God for You," 2.
61. Sumrall, *From Glory to Glory*, 64.

Canzenara of Jacksonville, Florida, who was on the team from Graham's organization. He showed Canzenara Graham's article in *Voice Magazine* and asked him if Graham was endorsing tongues. Canzenara was unsure of Graham's position, but he went on to witness to Sumrall of his own experience of being filled with the Spirit.[62] Even though Canzenara seemed filled with joy, Sumrall determined that it would not fit within the views of the Southern Baptist Convention.

While other individuals began coming into the experience of the baptism of the Holy Spirit, most were not interested because of their Baptist tradition. Sumrall felt increasingly frustrated with the situation at Boulevard Baptist. Ultimately the pressure became too much, and on January 1, 1964, he resigned to pursue a doctorate at New Orleans Baptist Theological Seminary.[63] He gave them sixty days to find his replacement. Moving on from the situation at Boulevard Baptist seemed to him his best option.

Two days later, F. E. Ward from Houston, Texas, called Sumrall. Ward had come to Pensacola to start a Full Gospel Business Men's Fellowship (FGBMF) chapter, and had a list of pastors in the area.[64] Ward invited him to his hotel room for a chat concerning the new ministry. Once there, Ward immediately began sharing with him about the baptism of the Holy Spirit and how the Lord was using FGBMF to introduce the fullness of the Spirit into people's lives. What amazed Sumrall was the news that this experience was happening with the Methodists, Presbyterians, and Catholics as well.[65] He pondered if this was the answer to the prayers he prayed during "The Hour of Power."

The next day Sumrall received a call from Pastor Dan Beasley, a Baptist minister from West Virginia. He was leading a revival service at Brownsville Assembly of God and called to invite him to attend. Having two perfect strangers call Sumrall in a matter of days persuaded him to go.[66] Again he heard what the Lord was doing all over the world in this newest move of the Spirit.[67] Afterwards, he and Beasley drove for coffee,

62. Ibid., 64–65.
63. Ibid., 65.
64. Ibid., 67.
65. Ibid., 66.
66. Ibid., 68–69.
67. See Full Gospel Business Men's Fellowship International, *Acts of the Holy Spirit among the Baptists Today*; *Acts of the Holy Spirit among the Methodists Today*; and *Acts of the Holy Spirit among the Presbyterians Today*.

and they talked for several hours. Intrigued, he visited Beasley in his motel room for the next two weeks. Finally, Sumrall asked God to baptize him with the Holy Spirit during one of his visits to Beasley's room. Nothing happened.[68] Beasley assured him that his time was coming and invited him to go with him to a FGBMF meeting in Houston the following week. He reluctantly agreed to go.

When they arrived, they were met at the airport by John Osteen. Osteen gave him a tour of his new church, but Sumrall was not impressed. They later attended the FGBMF meeting with Beasley, where Sumrall heard more testimonies of the baptism of the Holy Spirit. Afterwards, he returned to his motel room to pack for the trip home. He had to preach the next day at Boulevard. Before he could leave, Ward showed up at his door and prevailed upon him to stay one more night. Sumrall arranged for a substitute preacher, and he and Ward attended Pasadena Assembly of God that night.[69]

Pastor Goodwin of the church knew Ward and at one point in the service gave him an opportunity to lead the meeting. Ward called on Sumrall to come to the platform and simply walk around the altar. He complied, not really knowing why.[70] Next, Ward asked for everyone to get quiet because he felt that the Lord had a word for Sumrall. A hush fell over the room. Almost immediately, a woman in the congregation moved toward Sumrall while giving a message in tongues. Immediately Pastor Goodwin gave the interpretation. Upon hearing the interpretation, Sumrall felt his fears leave, and he began praising God. On February 9, 1964, he was baptized in the Spirit and began speaking in tongues.[71]

New Beginning of Liberty Church

Word had spread quickly of Sumrall's experience in Houston. Pastor Carl Arnold of Brownsville Assembly of God heard and asked him to share his testimony of the baptism of the Holy Spirit with his congregation.[72] But the local leadership of Boulevard Baptist had a different opinion, and they called a meeting with Sumrall that night.

---

68. Sumrall, *From Glory to Glory*, 69.
69. Ibid., 72–74.
70. Ibid., 75.
71. Sumrall, *Practical Church Government*, 13.
72. Sumrall, *From Glory to Glory*, 78.

At the deacons' meeting, the deacons expressed their concern that Ken's experience, while real, would destroy the church. Sumrall agreed. He suggested that he go ahead and leave and allow the deacons to explain what happened in whatever way they thought best.[73]

The next day at a FGBMF meeting Wanda received the baptism of the Spirit.[74] Soon afterward, Sumrall began receiving invitations to speak among Pentecostal and full gospel churches, as well at other FGBMF meetings. One unique meeting was at Springfield Community Church in Panama City, Florida. He had been invited to share his testimony concerning his baptism in the Spirit. During the sermon, he felt impressed to stop and wait. As he did a message in tongues was given. The interpretation was a powerfully directive word for him.[75] The central message was for Sumrall to not be afraid to begin a work in Pensacola. Many people were hungry for the Spirit's baptism, and if he would dedicate the work to the Lord he would enjoy God's favor.[76] For weeks prior he had been in a quandary over the direction he should take in the ministry.

Several couples in Pensacola were urging him to plant a church. However, Sumrall thought there were too many churches in Pensacola. But the prophetic word at Springfield had changed his perspective. He returned to Pensacola with confidence. Within days, he had located an empty storefront building for rent on Cervantes Street. Even though it was next to an ABC Liquor store, he was comfortable renting it. On March 16, 1964, he held his first service in the morning, with thirty-five people in attendance.[77] Fifty-one were in attendance later for the evening service. Within several weeks, the church had a hundred in attendance. He named the new church plant Liberty Baptist Church.[78] Nobody from the Southern Baptist Convention had bothered to ask him for his ordination papers, and since most of the folks were ex-Baptists, the name seemed appropriate at the time.[79]

---

73. Ibid., 79–80.

74. Ibid., 82.

75. Jackson, telephone interview with author, March 5, 2012. Donald is the son of the late Curtis Jackson, who was the assistant pastor at Springfield at the time.

76. Jackson, telephone interview with author, March 5, 2012. J. W. Hunt, who was the senior pastor at the time, interpreted the message in tongues for Sumrall.

77. Sumrall, *Practical Church Government*, 14.

78. Sumrall, *From Glory to Glory*, 88–89.

79. Ibid., 89.

Sumrall recorded several miracles during the early day of Liberty Baptist. But it soon became apparent that some structure was need for the new church plant. In the beginning he and the congregation wanted to be free from denominational rigidity. Some had a hard time adjusting to their newfound freedom, especially in worship and in the order of service. A demonstrative service was not within the Baptist paradigm. He had felt that anything organized was not free. So he approached the service with as little organization as possible.[80] There was no membership roll.

However, these new charismatic believers had no understanding on the correct use of the gifts. It was not uncommon for there to be nine messages in tongues during the service. Instead of flowing with the service, the prophetic words were, for Sumrall, irrelevant and most of the times extraneous. Problems continued. Frequently visitors would have someone prophesying over them before they could take a seat.[81]

Sumrall turned to two trusted friends for advice, Ralph Branham and Charles Simpson, who were fellow Spirit-filled Baptist pastors. They met regularly and prayed for guidance and direction for Sumrall. At their encouragement and admonishment, he determined to faithfully teach the biblical use of the gifts of the Spirit. As he tried to bring a biblical balance to the use of the gifts, people began to leave. From the high attendance of 101, the church had lost over half of the people. Ironically, this exodus occurred as the church was trying to purchase a small tract of land on 57th Avenue in Pensacola.[82]

With the lease running out on the storefront on Cervantes Street, Sumrall moved ahead with the remaining faithful attendees and sold enough church bonds to purchase the land and build a 34x125-foot concrete block structure for their new sanctuary.[83] This new facility had seating for 200 people. Liberty Baptist Church was ready for growth. But the expansion would be much larger than one church could hold. In time, Sumrall would lead a network of churches—Liberty Fellowship of Churches and Ministers.

---

80. Sumrall, *Practical Church Government*, 15.
81. Sumrall, *From Glory to Glory*, 103–6.
82. Ibid., 106–8.
83. Ibid., 111.

4

Liberty Fellowship of Churches and Ministers: Movement or Institution?

AT THE ZENITH OF Liberty Bible College, which was a visionary result from Sumrall's desire to train future church leaders, graduating students were finding their place in a variety of ministries. These included senior pastors, associated pastors, worship leaders, youth pastors, and missionaries. Feeling a close camaraderie with their school and with Sumrall, they began to ask for an association or fellowship for spiritual encouragement and guidance.[1] Many voiced their opinion that Sumrall was the leader whom they desired as the vanguard for their respected ministries.[2] Sumrall understood their request as part of the new work God was seeking to establish through the charismatic movement. In July 1975, twenty-one ministers who had graduated from Liberty Bible College met to discuss and write the founding charter for Liberty Fellowship of Churches and Ministers (LFCM). There was a consensus amongst them that there was a genuine need for some sort of written agreement for those who would be working closely together in the work of the Lord. Additionally, the written agreement would be vital for those who would inquire concerning what LFCM believed and how the fellowship worked.[3]

During this decade, others within the charismatic renewal movement were also contemplating similar decisions. The charismatic renewal catapulted the emergence of the basic Pentecostal experience with its gifts of the Spirit, but its development when beyond the recognized boundaries of the Pentecostal movement. At its early stage the charismatic renewal

---

1. Kelly, interview with author, May 12, 2012.
2. Stamps, interview with author, August 9, 2012.
3. Sumrall, *New Wine Bottles*, 191.

developed into two streams of thought. First was the renewal movement within older denominations and churches. Second was the rise of new charismatic churches, which included ministries and, later, networks outside of and unconnected with older denominations or the Pentecostal movement.[4] Donald Gee commented about denominational loyalties in foreseeing the growth of the Pentecostal phenomenon:

> before we became so Movement-conscious we thought more often of the Pentecostal Revival as a means of grace to quicken whomsoever the Lord our God should call. Denominational loyalties were a secondary consideration. Let them remain such. The vital necessity of the Movement is that it shall continue and grow as a Revival. Nothing less deserves to be called 'Pentecostal.'[5]

Gee would add years later that "Pentecost is more than a denomination; it is a REVIVAL."[6] The independent sector of the charismatic renewal was welcomed neither by Pentecostals nor by the renewal currents within historic churches. The suspicion of the newer leadership of the charismatic renewal was to not become like the older Pentecostal movement. For them, the Pentecostal churches reflected the extent to which the Pentecostal movement had become institutionalized or denominationalized. The historical churches were concerned that the charismatic renewal lacked accountability and were concerned over their deviant teachings. As more and more independent charismatic churches were birthed, the historical churches saw this "come out" position as "outside," a deviation from the norm or the ideal that church history upheld, especially with its restorationist emphasis on the spiritual gifts and the fivefold ministries of Ephesians 4.[7]

For Sumrall, the charismatic renewal and LFCM were much more than an updating or adaptation of the Pentecostal movement. It was much more than "coming out" because of one's disdain for the lack of openness to the charismata. There was a bigger picture. He believed that the Spirit of God was developing a new type of governmental structure that required a "new wineskin" for directing the church. LFCM represented a development going beyond what was already present in the Pentecostal movement. What was common for the Pentecostal movement in patterns of ministry and

---

4. Hockens, *Challenges of the Pentecostal, Charismatic, and Messianic Jewish Movements*, 29.

5. Gee, "Are We Too 'Movement' Conscious?," 5.

6. Gee, "Tongues and Truth," 7.

7. Hockens, "Charismatic Movement," 516.

organization was to be surpassed by the "restoration" of apostolic and prophetic ministries.[8] Sumrall maintained that the New Testament principles of apostolic government be restored and practiced in order for the glory of God to fully return to the body of Christ.[9] If not, his fear was that the church would deteriorate into as ineffective institution.

Institutionalization

At the beginning of LFCM, Sumrall was not necessarily against Liberty Fellowship becoming a new Christian organization or denomination. He maintained that one centralized organization under the same administration tended towards staleness and stagnation,[10] while many flexible extra-local organizations, each one setting its own rules of conduct and whose apostolic leaders communicated with each other, would promote stability and maturity in the kingdom of God.[11] Organizations or denominations were not evil in Sumrall's view. The issue for him was that churches and people moved from a living organism of the faith to a dead organization because generations after the move of God they did not have the convictions of their founders. The result was that organizations start to exist for themselves and their own preservation. This was not the avenue for the desired restorationism toward which Sumrall aimed. The church of the first century was to function as a kind of *pars pro toto*, a community for the sake of all others, a model for others to emulate and by which to be challenged. But it was never to sever itself from others.[12] If not, then its survival as a religious group, rather than its commitment to the reign of God, would begin to preoccupy it.[13] Lamenting this outcome, Sumrall advanced that the focus should be on the kingdom of God and restoring a New Testament pattern for governing the church.

Without the restoration of the New Testament paradigm, the church would cease to be a movement and turn into an institution. History has

---

8. Sumrall, *Practical Church Government*, 17–18.
9. Sumrall, *New Wine Bottles*, 40.
10. Ibid., 55.
11. At this point, Sumrall had not fully developed his understanding of apostolic government, especially the relational aspect of "fathers" (i.e. apostles) leading each extra-local congregation.
12. Bosch, *Transforming Mission*, 50.
13. Loisy, *Gospel and the Church*, xxxvii–xlii.

revealed essential differences between these two. One was conservative; the other was progressive. One yielded to the influences from the outside world, thereby becoming passive; the other was operative, influencing rather than being influenced. One looked to the past, while the other looked toward the future. One guarded the boundaries, while the other crossed them.[14] An example of this comparison between an institution and a movement can be found between the Christian community in Jerusalem with that of Antioch in the first century. The pioneering spirit of the Antioch church precipitated an inspection by Jerusalem. Jerusalem was not concerned with mission and movement but with consolidation. The apostolic council of Acts 15 and Paul's statements in Galatians 2 pointed to the tendency in the early church to become an institution. Two separate styles of ministries seemed to be developing: the settled ministry of bishops, elders, and deacons, and the mobile ministry of apostles, prophets, and evangelists. Sumrall maintained that the charismatic renewal was a movement where the Lord was restoring important New Testament principles of apostolic government to the body of Christ.[15]

Ralph Winter stated, "Every major decision you make will be faulty until you see the whole world as God sees it."[16] Sumrall embraced this thought and fully believed that the church that Jesus desired was to be designed with built-in, self-generative capacities and was made for nothing less than world-transforming, lasting, and revolutionary impact. Christianity was never meant to become a domesticated civil religion. Any infertility of the church arose from within the community of faith. In fact, sociologists have long acknowledged that decline in the church was associated with ever-encroaching doubt.[17] It heralded impending fruitlessness and decline in the people of God. One only has to recall the cycle of disintegration and renewal in the accounts of the Old Testament.

First, this doubt in the life cycle of a movement was operational. The organization labored to keep pace with its missional purpose. The problem centered on the wineskin or governmental structure. In short, its organizational systems and designs formally used to advance the founding ideas were no longer adequate for the job. If this problem of wineskin was not

---

14. Niebuhr, *Kingdom of God in America*, 11–13.
15. Sumrall, *New Wine Bottles*, 40.
16. Hawthrone, "Perspectives," 28, as quoted in Ahrend, *In This Generation*, 172.
17. Kelly, *Why Conservative Churches Are Growing*, 56–96. Kelly maintains that social and moral strengths and leniency do not blend well within a church or movement.

solved, the community of faith would enter into cynicism and unbelief or ideological doubt. The individuals or people no longer believed the message itself. The next phrase was ethical doubt, where people's behavior no longer lined up with the mandate of the vision. Last was absolute doubt, which hastens closure and the death of the original movement.[18]

Sumrall held that the charismatic renewal was a movement that required believers to adapt to God's intentions for the church and the world. He postulated that Scripture taught an extra-local oversight of churches and ministries rather than local autonomy of independent churches. Each must come under the authority of an apostle and its elders.[19] Consequently, he advanced a new paradigm for ministry.

However, the parallel between paradigms and institutionalization is that, once established, paradigms in many ways tend to do our thinking for us. As they develop, we unsuspectingly developed an algorithm. An algorithm comes from one's rational process, which helps one' produce reliable outcomes. While such an algorithm is reliable, one can be overpowered by circumstances when the future no longer resembles the past.[20] While helping one to make sense of the world, it can also create paradigm blindness—the incapacity to see issues from outside a particular perspective.[21] When the context shifts considerably, the algorithm can be dubious because it prevents an organization from seeing its way forward. The church must innovate, keep learning, and be resilient and adaptive. Sumrall suggested that this learning would lead one to embrace extra-local oversight of apostles and elders.

Organizations need definable social roles (elders and deacons) and need to proclaim what is valued and standardized (ethics). They create rites and liturgies in an attempt to maintain the transmission of the message to generations that follow. Hence, they develop institutions and traditions that are intended to help preserve the faith beyond the first generation. Maier, a biblical historian, advanced that while Paul was still living, the process of institutionalization was in its early stages. Time, the growth of the group, the absence of the apostle Paul, and the action of certain members

---

18. Adapted from Cada et al., *Shaping the Coming Age of Religious Life*, 53, 78.
19. Sumrall, *New Wine Bottles*, 118–19.
20. Martin, *Design of Business*, 43.
21. Hirsch and Ferguson, *On the Verge*. This book unpacks paradigm blindness and its relationship to how we understand the church.

all encouraged the development of organizational systems.[22] James D. G. Dunn stated that the consequence was the spreading of institutionalism. The church progressively connected with the external forms of the institution itself.

> Increasing institutionalization is the clearest mark of early Catholicism—when church becomes increasingly identified with institution, when authority becomes increasingly coterminous with office, when a basic distinction between clergy and laity becomes increasingly self-evident, when grace becomes increasingly narrowed to well-defined ritual acts. . . . such features were absent from [later] generations the picture was beginning to change.[23]

Thomas O'Dea agreed. A Catholic sociologist, he posited that to survive its charismatic beginnings, the movement must become stable through forms and policies. However, he underscored that this desire to capture the sacred creates a certain paradox because the ultimate and the sacred cannot be enclosed in organizational structures without those systems taking on a life of their own. If so, they corrupt what they were intended to preserve.[24] More pointedly, the charismatic/Pentecostal hermeneutical core has experience as a main ontological underpinning,[25] especially the experience of the supernatural and the gifts of the Spirit. Since its religious experience was spontaneous and creative, and since institutionalization required reducing these unpredictable elements to established and rote forms,[26] the dilemma was one of great importance for Sumrall's restorationism.

As such, there developed an irresolvable dilemma that exists for any organization, especially for religious ones. The charismatic renewal was born out of firsthand religious experience through the rediscovery of the charismata and the baptism of the Holy Spirit. For the movement to grow and prosper there was some need for stability and order. The charisma (grace gift) needed to be distributed and settled by the organization so that the initial gift(s) of the founder or movement could be accessible throughout the organization itself. O'Dea understood the process of institutionalization as not only inevitable, but necessary. Paradoxically, this process may

---

22. Maier, *Social Setting of the Ministry*, 39.
23. Dunn, *Unity and Diversity in the New Testament*, 351.
24. O'Dea, "Five Dilemmas in the Institutionalization of Religion," 31–32.
25. See Goldingay, *Models for Interpretation of Scripture*; Archer, *Pentecostal Hermeneutic for the Twenty-First Century*; and Thorsen, *Wesleyan Quadrilateral*.
26. Ibid.

well dilute or destroy the initial passion and message of the founder and the movement. The crisis surfaced when the outward forms of worship no longer aligned with the inward experience from which the movement was birthed. Decline was the result. The authentic passion of the movement was supplanted and constant renewal became necessary. The need to re-Jesus the movement became obligatory.[27]

Outcomes of Institutionalization

Unchecked, institutionalization regresses into the need to retain, control, and direct the initial passion and direction of the original movement. It can easily slip into a conscious (or unconscious) attempt to domesticate and mediate God, his Spirit, and his kingdom. Institutionalization can readily lapse into institutionalism. Unbridled, the church or any fellowship of churches can become an idol.

Another possible issue with the institutionalization of the movement is the literature it created. New writings and new ideas were a definitive sign that a movement was taking place. One only needs to think of the volumes that have been written about the Pentecostal/charismatic movement to agree with this axiom. While it needed those manuscripts, when they are separated from their original context, there can be a tendency to displace the people who started it.[28] In other words, the ideas of the original movement can deteriorate into mere ideology. Ideology can create ideologues who can be controlling and abusive. Hence, there seems to be a constant need for renewal and relegitimization.[29] Theological ideas should inform and influence one's relationship with God. While ideas are very important, they should point to and from where they came. Hence, ideas serve a greater reality. Sumrall endeavored to counter this displacement by emphasizing the need for community within the restoration process.[30]

Bureaucracy is another routine in the process of institutionalization. Unless movements become very intentional about their passions and message, they tend towards a state of equilibrium. Organizations become progressively internally centered and take less risk. The need for security

---

27. Frost and Hirsch, *ReJesus*, 77.

28. For insights into how social context is paramount for information and ideas see Brown and Duguid, *Social Life of Information*.

29. This is the main emphasis of Frost and Hirsch's book, *ReJesus*.

30. Sumrall, *New Wine Bottles*, 43.

and safety begins to dominate and shapes the leadership. Peter Berger, a religious sociologist, described this process as bureaucratization. In this progression, the organization selects leadership that will best cater to the felt need of the organization (or church). Bureaucracies demand these types of personnel.

> This personnel is specific not only in terms of its functions and requisite skills, but also in terms of its psychological characteristics. Institutions both *select* and *form* the personnel they require for their operation. This means that similar . . . types of leadership emerge in the various religious institutions, irrespective of the traditional patterns in this matter. . . . [The leader] must above all adapt himself to the requirements of his bureaucratic role.[31]

Hence, bureaucracies increasingly become more selective and enlarged systems. Unless resisted, leadership becomes more and more bureaucratic in outlook. However, the uncontrollable pneumatic aspect of the Book of Acts seems to fly in the face of this human urge to control or set limits. The disciples were entrusted with the mission of Jesus, which moved beyond their temple theology or ethnocentric understanding of the gospel. This pneumatocracy,[32] the uncontrollable rule and guidance of the Spirit of God, highlights the conflict between bureaucracies and the people of the Spirit. Sumrall taught that humanity was created to have fellowship with God and the Holy Spirit. Thereby they have a void in their lives for the supernatural. Christianity, for Sumrall, was supernatural from its very first day, and it will be supernatural until the last day.[33]

The last distinctive feature that advanced institutionalization in the early church was the substitution of apostolic doctrine for the active, living ministry of an apostle. With the inclusion of the Gentiles, many theological controversies developed in the church during the first-century. The apostles dealt with issues of legalism, Jewish nationalism, Gnosticism, and other ideologies. As the church grew, it expanded in its non-Jewish context. This development into non-Jewish growth created issues that would need addressing—the canon of Scripture, the nature of God, Trinity, and Christology, just to name a few. Orthodoxy became the driving force for the church. To survive these heretical threats, leaders underscored the need for fixed,

---

31. Berger, *Sacred Canopy*, 139–40.

32. Hirsch and Catchim, *Permanent Revolution*, 263. I am indebted to Alan Hirsch for this terminology.

33. Sumrall, *Confidence*, 59.

legitimate, and authoritative sources of doctrine. The writings of the New Testament apostles became the cornerstone upon which the canon was built. It later became known as the apostolic faith.[34] Orthodoxy became the driving concern for the church. The codification and standardization of belief and action was used to survive the threat of heresy. This nature of doctrine justified the abrogation of the apostolic function and office in the church.

This bend towards doctrinal purity and church polity, which was obviously needed, shifted the church from being mission-minded to being a more defensive and self-referential community of believers. As a result of the departure of the apostolic function, several issues resulted. First, leadership became maintenance-minded. As such, the driving missional emphasis was displaced. Second, there was movement away from the decentralized networking associated with apostolic endeavors. The church embraced a more centralized authority of bishops and elders, who favored a more hierarchical, bureaucratic, and conforming style of church government.[35] This movement away from the apostle revealed that that ministry was eclipsed by the local, increasingly maintenance-oriented leadership of bishops, elders, and deacons.

Moving away from the foundational, pioneering, extra-local, and custodial leadership of the apostles was costly. Local Christian communities (modalities), which were birthed by apostolic pioneers (sodalities), rejected their capacity to achieve and perpetuate the apostolic movement. Ed Stetzer, a missiologist, pointed out, "When the Reformers (and later evangelicals) deemphasized the apostolic nature of the church, they inadvertently lessened the sending nature of that apostolic church. The church that 'reformed' lost touch with the God who sends, and the mission of the church suffered."[36] Today in America, those without a religious identity have risen to one in five adults, resulting in the Protestant denomination losing its majority status.[37] The official exile from the church is very real. We are in a legitimate post-Christian culture. The need to recover the apostolic imagination and practice is paramount as well as the urgency to identify and change the sociopolitical dynamics of the institutionalization process.

---

34. Bruce, *Canon of Scripture*, 260.
35. Campbell, *Elders*, 216–35.
36. Stetzer, *Planting Missional Churches*, 29.
37. Grossman, "Protestants Lose Majority Status in U.S."

Is Institutionalization Avoidable?

However, we must ask ourselves whether institutionalization is avoidable. Is it fair to expect a movement to survive only as a movement? Sociological insight tends to support that a movement either disintegrates or becomes an institution. Historically, religious groups that began out of a movement and managed to survive did so because they gradually institutionalized. The Waldensians, the Moravians, the Quakers, and the Pentecostals are just a few examples. Movements have usually been birthed by individuals who were on the periphery of the church structure. The point is that few people can be both on the fringe and in the center at the same time.

It cannot be both ways—purely and exclusively a religious movement, yet at the same time something that will survive the centuries and continue to exercise a dynamic influence. Paul Pierson, a missiologist, maintained that God's redemptive mission has been worked out in history through the normative use of two structures: modalities and sodalities. Modalities or church structures can be defined as structured fellowships in which membership is broadly inclusive. They provide overall unity, continuity, and longevity. They ensure stability and serve as a resource base. Moreover, they give the necessary checks and balances between unbridled initiative and power-hungry bureaucracy. They offer authority and authenticity and consolidate Christianity upon its expansion. Sodalities or church mission structures can be defined as structured fellowships in which membership involve an adult second decision beyond membership of the modality. They provide stimulation of new life and innovation, as well as introducing diversity. They plan for mobility and expansion and major on in-depth commitment and gospel patterns. They render opportunity to expand to new territories and focus on special needs or tasks.[38] Throughout Christian expansion, it seems that sodalities have been used to expand the church into new territories, while modalities have tended to consolidate the church once it has taken root. Pierson asserted that the Christian movement has its best potential for expansion when modalities and sodalities are symbiotically related to one another to accomplish their functions.[39]

The point of objection should be, not that a movement becomes an institution, but that it loses much of its passion and zeal. When the ardent

---

38. Winter, "Two Structures of God's Redemptive Mission." Pierson was greatly influenced by Ralph Winter.

39. Pierson, "Historical Development of the Christian Movement," 16–18.

convictions of its first adherents cool down and become crystalized codes of petrified dogma, institutionalization results. The prophet becomes the priest of the bureaucracy, the charisma becomes an office, and love becomes routine. The horizon is no longer the world but the boundaries of the local church. Time tames the original passion of its beginnings into a still-flowing rivulet that eventually becomes a stationary pond. In fact, Sumrall stated that "in two more generations Liberty Fellowship could be guilty of the same and succumb to an ecclesiastical hierarchy spirit and political ladder-climbing."[40] Hence the question becomes: Which one is the driving force in the movement or institution—the structure (modality) or the mission (sodality)? Does the modality serve the sodality, or does the sodality serve the modality? How these questions were answered would determine if LFCM would remain a movement that was viable and passionate.

Governmental Church Structure—Fivefold Ministry

If the church was to not concede to a passionless hierarchy, Sumrall believed that a genuine theocracy was needed to restore the church. Simply put, with the restoration of New Testament power and love through the charismatic renewal, there must be a restoration of God's divine order in government. For Sumrall, this reclamation would be administered in the church through Holy Spirit-chosen and anointed men. These individuals would be gifted according to Eph 4:11–12—fivefold ministers. Sumrall firmly believed that the fivefold ministers were part of God's divine restoration of the charismatic renewal and God's divine order for church government.[41] Sumrall held that if one heard what the Spirit is saying to the churches concerning divine order in the body of Christ as it is written in God's Word, the glory of the Lord (with all its manifestations presented in the Book of Acts) would return to the church.[42] Without this biblical order, the charismatic renewal and LFCM would reach a plateau and disintegrate.

Moreover, Sumrall maintained that New Testament government was patterned after the theocracy of the Old Testament. Submission to the authority of God was expressed by submission to his delegated leadership. He particularly emphasized the plurality of eldership.[43] Moreover, he held

---

40. Sumrall, *New Wine Bottles*, 50.
41. Ibid., 59–62.
42. Ibid., 39.
43. Sumrall, *Apostolic Fathers and Their Families*, 19–22. He cited Rom 15:4; 1 Cor

that the seventy elders/leaders who helped Moses lead the people of God became the Sanhedrin during the life of Jesus. However, because of the Jew's refusal to embrace the rule of the kingdom, it was given to another nation—the church. Where Jesus Christ ruled his church through his delegated authority, there was pure theocracy.[44] Sumrall held that apostolic government needed to be restored and practiced in order for the glory of God to fully return to the body of Christ. Moreover, for the church to function in power there must be a sense of mutual dependence, especially worked out in community through relationships.[45]

Governmentally, these relationships were exercised in the church through the fivefold ministers working as a team. This allowed for a blending of gifts, talents, and personalities as the vision of the church provided for leadership to grow through its relationships.[46] In fact, it was a part of LFCM's doctrinal statement. In it Sumrall outlined their position on the ordained officers of the church:

> The ordained officers of the Church are apostle, prophet, evangelist, pastor, teacher, local (counseling) elders and deacons (Ephesians 4:11; 1 Timothy 3; Titus 1:5–9). Apostles, prophets, evangelists, pastors, and teachers shall not necessarily all function in one local church. However, it is believed that all of these officers shall function under the covering of a local church and all local (counseling) elders are under the supervision of the fivefold ministry listed in Ephesians 4:11 (Acts 15; 1 Timothy 5:17–21; Titus 1:5–9).[47]

All LFCM had to adopt the same articles of faith, but the local church could set their own bylaws for church membership.

Sumrall maintained that extra-local authority was the rational link that held the New Testament church together. Paul's letters revealed that he had apostolic oversight that extended beyond the local church. As such, Sumrall understood that some leaders were given charge beyond the local church. These extra-local leaders were from the fivefold ministry of Eph

---

10:11; Exod 18:13–26 and Num 11:16–17 as scriptural evidence for his convictions.

44. Sumrall, *New Wine Bottles*, 27–30.

45. Sumrall would develop the relationship aspect of church government with the birthing of Church Foundational Network. At this time in his life, the relational feature of apostolic government was still forming in his thinking.

46. Sumrall, *New Wine Bottles*, 40–45.

47. Ibid., 100.

4:11–12. For Sumrall there was wisdom in a fellowship of churches that had oversight from the same administration.[48]

Apostolic Challenge

The rediscovery and reapplication of this one strategy of Pauline ecclesiology had massive consequences for the present-day charismatic movement. This highly transformative apostolic movement has achieved significant missional impact through some expression of the fivefold ministry. Alan Hirsch posited that this missional progress comes from what he called "the apostolic genius."[49] Compared to human DNA, the apostolic genius was the simple, intrinsic, central guiding mechanism that gave sustainability and growth to kingdom of God. It was the life force that pulsated through the New Testament church and throughout church history.[50] Hirsch admitted that the term was unusual, but he posited that it was "the total phenomenon resulting from a complex of multiform and real experiences of God, types of expression, organizational structures, leadership ethos, spiritual power, mode of belief, etc. And it is the active presence, or the lack of it, that makes all the difference to our experience of Jesus community, mission, and spiritual power."[51] As such, there was no substantial word for this missional and catalytic power other than the biblical word *apostolic*.[52] *Apostolic* was not just about the power of the gospel or about apostolic doctrine, but about a specific type of leadership and, more pointedly, about an apostolic person. Sumrall, however, would underscore leadership as an apostolic team, which was made up of the fivefold ministers.[53]

To recover the apostolic genius, there needed to be a redress in the church—a going back to our founder and resetting our faith and communal life on him. This would re-engage the central confession of "Jesus is Lord." It meant simplifying our core message, unpacking our complex theologies,

---

48. Ibid., 109–24.
49. Hirsch, *Forgotten Ways*, 75–82.
50. Ibid., 77.
51. Ibid., 78.
52. Garrison, *Church Planting Movements*, 17. Instead of using the term "apostolic," Garrison calls these individuals "strategy coordinators."
53. Sumrall, *Practical Church Government*, 30. Later, Sumrall would see church government in a "family" paradigm with apostles defined as spiritual fathers. See chapter 5.

and examining our traditional templates for ministry. Lee Camp underscored this need in his book on discipleship:

> The proclamation of the "gospel" has often failed to emphasize a fundamental element of the teaching of Jesus, and indeed, of orthodox Christian doctrine: "Jesus is Lord" is a radical claim, one that is ultimately rooted in questions of allegiance, of ultimate authority, of the ultimate norm and standard for human life. Instead, Christianity has often sought to ally itself comfortably with allegiance to other authorities, be they political, economic, cultural, or ethnic. Could it be that "Jesus is Lord" has become one of the most widespread Christian lies?[54]

What is needed is an unencumbered Christology of the New Testament church, as this lies at the heart of the renewal of the church throughout history. God's people can obscure the centrality of Jesus in our experience of church. The confession "Jesus is Lord" was to take seriously the absolute centrality of Jesus in one's view of the church and the kingdom of God. The first step in recovering the apostolic genius was to recover the lordship of Jesus in all its utter simplicity.

Another major challenge for the fivefold ministry to operate in the church was what Alan Roxburgh called liminality. In his understanding, liminality was the transition from one fundamental form of the church to another, which necessitated the apostolic role.[55] What Sumrall embraced concerning the fivefold ministry would require change for most church leaders. The situation required a pioneering and innovative mode of leadership to help the church adapt to this new paradigm. Roxburgh went on to posit that the predominately pastoral conception of the church and ministry, in reality, constituted a major hindrance to the church reconceiving itself with an apostolic emphasis. Moreover, he stated that, in relation to the institutionalization and dominance of the pastoral function embodied in ordination, the guild of the ordained would need to be restructured, especially in light of the other fivefold gifts. This one gift of the church would not move the church through liminality.[56]

Following on this point, it is fair to ask: why would Paul, in Eph 2:20, state that the church was built on the foundation of the apostles and

---

54. Camp, *Mere Discipleship*, 16.

55. Roxburgh, *Missionary Congregation, Leadership and Liminality*, 61.

56. Ibid., 64–65. Sumrall believed that the modern-day apostle would facilitate this transitional change for the church, especially for a new apostolic governmental structure.

prophets? Sumrall maintained that the apostolic ministry provided both the environment and the reference point for the other ministries mentioned in Scripture.[57] Roxburgh stated that the apostolic ministry was "foundational to all other functions."[58] In other words, it initiated the other ones and constituted their foundation. The apostolic ministry was rooted and disseminated among the other ministries that form the fivefold ministry of Ephesians 4. Hence one could postulate that the apostolic ministry created the environment for the prophetic, the prophetic created the environment for the evangelistic, and so forth.[59] All five ministries were needed to generate, awaken, and nurture the full ministry of the church. All five ministries in progressive relation to one another were decisively vital to true discipleship and healthy and growing movements.

Part of the resistance to the rise of the apostolic ministry/movement was that at times people who have claimed an apostolic anointing have had a dictatorial approach to leadership. What resulted was a disempowering of the people, who remained immature and powerless and who were dependent upon an autocratic form of church government. Sumrall insisted that the title of apostle did not denote superiority, but responsibility. Additionally, apostolic ministry worked in and through a team. He flatly denied an autocratic form of church government (i.e., one-man rule of the church) but firmly believed that God's plan was for the church to be led by a plurality of leaders who served under/with an apostolic leader.[60] Fivefold leadership was based upon inspiration and passion. Moreover, fivefold leaders and their followers provoked each other to higher levels of godliness and spirituality by engaging in shared values, callings, and identity. The relationship was opened where each influences the other by pursuit of common objectives, especially with the aim of allowing followers to become leaders in their own passions.[61] In short, fivefold leaders called others to greatness. They were charged to develop the gifts and callings of all of God's people. It

---

57. Sumrall, *New Wine Bottles*, 127–39.

58. Roxburgh, *Missionary Congregation*, 62.

59. McQuarrie *Principles of Christian Theology*, 391. Even the office gift of the bishop serves as a steward to the apostolic and is viewed as "having in himself all the other ministries," which are conferred to others through ordination. With the bishop, Christendom quenched the pioneer aspect of the faith and institutionalized apostolicity in the church and office. Doing so, it reshaped it into a more distinctly pastoral image so as to comply with the diocesan context.

60. Sumrall, *Practical Church Government*, 51.

61. Hirsch, *Forgotten Ways*, 159–60.

involved empowerment. In fact, dominant, charismatic leaders oftentimes become one of the greatest hindrances to any church/organization from moving from being good to becoming great.[62]

The Apostolic and the Issue of Cessationism

The reality for Sumrall was that the Ephesians 4 typology was a major piece of Pauline ecclesiology, and LFCM was to be patterned after it. He called for an open-minded and focused thinking on this passage of Scripture, even though there has been mostly silence or misunderstanding on its emphasis for church government. Sumrall recognized that there has been a deeply ingrained belief that somehow Ephesians 4 no longer applied to the church. However, in Ephesians 4 Paul was specifically speaking about the ecclesia as God intended it to function. Markus Barth called this passage of Scripture the "Constitution of the Church."[63] This passage gave constitutional weight for Sumrall's thinking, and as such it helped to set the criteria of how one must think about church government and the essential framework by which it was intended to operate. It was the interpretive center of how Sumrall conceived of ministry.

The problem has been that the church did not completely embrace the idea of the apostle, the prophet, and to some degree the evangelist. The major leader for the church was the pastor. The pastor became the organizing center for determining what was normal for church government and, thereby, what was not normal. The apostle, the prophet, and the evangelist were discarded from the church's organizational structure. If the church continued to use the standard of pastor and teacher as the frameworks for the ministry of the church, then its primary purpose would be to run worship services and Bible studies. However, Sumrall maintained that the fivefold ministries had paradigmatic significance for the church as it fulfilled its mission in the world. The consequences of reducing the leadership structure of the church to just pastor and teacher have been demonstrated through the history of the church.

Limiting church leadership to just the gifts of pastor and teacher had a procrustean effect which has set a standard by which everything else was subsequently forced to conform. It meant positing a set of suppositions for leadership even when they did not fit. Hence, having exiled the apostolic,

---

62. Collins, *Good to Great*, 65–89.
63. Barth, *Ephesians*, 425.

the prophetic, and the evangelistic gifts from the church, the other two retrofitted the facts and evidence into pre-existing categories so as to resolve categorical tensions. For example Arthur Patzia, a New Testament scholar, stated that Christ gave the fivefold offices to the church so that the church might reach its full maturity. But he went on to state that the gifts of apostle, prophet, and evangelist were replaced by the canon of Scripture and the role of the pastor and teacher.[64]

Moreover, John Calvin made the following observation concerning the fivefold ministers mentioned in Ephesians 4:

> According to this interpretation, . . . these three (apostles, prophets, and evangelist) functions were not established in the church as permanent ones, but only for that time during which churches were to be erected where none existed before, or where they were to be carried over from Moses to Christ. Still, I do not deny that the Lord has sometimes at a later period raised up apostles, or at least evangelists in their place, as has happened in our day. For these was need for such persons to lead the church back from the rebellion of Antichrist. Nonetheless, I call this office "extraordinary," because in duly constituted churches it has no place.[65]

Alan Roxburgh acknowledged the emphasis of the fivefold typology in Ephesians 4. However, he incorporated the apostolic and prophetic functions into that of the pastor. In fact, he included all the fivefold gifts into the role of the pastor. There was no legitimate place for the prophet or apostle.[66]

These opinions underscore the significance of one's exegetical position of the Ephesian 4 pericope. At issue is where one places the comma in verse 12. The RSV, NIV, NKJV, NASB, and NEB all have omitted a comma in verse 12, hence the verse states, "for the equipping of the saints for the work of ministry, for the edifying of the body of Christ (HCSB)." The KJV (and the RSV of 1946) place the commas between the prepositional phrases of verse 12. They read, "for the perfecting of the saints, for the work of the ministry, for the edifying of the body of Christ." Omitting the comma after the first prepositional phrase became standard practice ever since the publication of the NEB in 1961. Moreover, Luther did not use a comma in

---

64. Patzia, *Ephesians, Colossians, Philemon*, 216–18.
65. Calvin, *Institutes of the Christian Religion*, 2:1057.
66. Roxburgh, "Missional Leadership."

his translation of 1534.[67] Joseph A. Robinson[68] and Markus Barth[69] both omitted the comma in their commentaries of the text. The autographs of the New Testament, of course, contained no punctuation, so placing a comma did not involve tampering with the original text. Beginning with the publication of the NEB in 1961, the newer translation rapidly became the standard translation and has so ever since.[70] The question became whether Eph 4:12 taught that the ministry of the church was done by the saints or by the office gifts of the apostle, prophet, evangelist, pastor, and teacher.[71]

Sumrall understood the reality of the priesthood of the believer, but he did not hold to the clergyhood of believers. The restoration of the charismata within the church would be characterized by a revival of appreciating the ministry of the word and the ministry of the sacraments or ordinances by ordained ministers. He held that each member was to recognize God's appointed ministers and submit to them in the Lord, as these ministers oversee them in love. In LFMC, Sumrall taught that the fivefold ministries (apostle, prophet, evangelist, pastor, and teacher) were office gifts for the church.[72]

Taking Sumrall's position, the Ephesians 4 text would be understood as Jesus equipping some in the body with the fivefold gifts so as to train all others do to ministry. In short, the church staff equipped the members to do the ministry. This has been the standard, institutional way that the church has organized itself. However, if one reads the Eph 4:7–12 organically, then grace has been given to "each and every person." Hence, rather than these gifts being given to an elite few for the equipping of many, these gifts were given to all and for the benefit of all. It was the saints equipping the saints.[73] Additionally, Ephesians was addressed to "the saints at Ephesus," which included men, women, slaves, and all the nonprofessional type of believers. Paul's hearers came from a very broad spectrum across racial, social, economic, and gender lines. Hence, the fivefold ministries would fit all believers. All believers would come to the church with their gifts and provide for the continual development of the movement. This paradigm of ministry would underscore that the fundamental ministry of the church

---

67. Secker, "Ephesians 4:11–12 Reconsidered," 59–60.
68. Robinson, *St. Paul's Epistle to the Ephesians*, 103.
69. Barth, *Ephesians*, 479.
70. Secker, "Ephesians 4:11–12 Reconsidered," 59.
71. Gordon, "'Equipping' Ministry in Ephesians 4?," 70.
72. Sumrall, *New Wine Bottles*, 100.
73. Hirsch and Catchim, *Permanent Revolution*, 21.

was charismatic and that Ephesians 4 was not necessarily a leadership text but a ministry text. Accordingly, the emphasis of the fivefold ministry would shift from the notion of office to that of function.[74]

The fivefold ministry would be part of the DNA of all believers and at the heart of what it means to be the church. It would be implicit. Leadership's central task would be to build a fivefold, charismatically empowered, ministering community of believers based upon Eph 4:11–12.[75] Leadership, thereby, would differ from calling and ministry only by degree and capacity. Hence, the leadership structure of the church becomes two-dimensional: a leadership matrix and a ministry matrix. This is not to disregard Paul's instructions for elders/deacons within the local church. But the fivefold ministers would embody a type of "calling within the calling."[76] It would revolve around a set of skills that augments the basic calling and influences of others from within that call. It was with this fresh perspective that Sumrall envisioned the restoration that the Lord was doing in the charismatic renewal, which required a new structure of church government. However, his view of leadership was more hierarchical than organic.

Implementation and Results

In 1975 LFCM was formed as an extra-local authority for the purpose of serving as an ordaining council for ministers, as advisors to pastors, and as presiding elders of LFCM in legal and spiritual affairs. The presbytery was made up from individuals who were recognized as operating in one of the fivefold gifts of Eph 4:11–12.[77] Liberty Church of Pensacola, Florida, was considered the mother church for LFMC. As such, its function and authority was looked upon with more regard than the other churches within the fellowship.[78] The fellowship was divided into geographical regions, with a member of the presbytery in authority of that district. Monthly meetings were held for all ministers and churches for the purpose of teaching and

---

74. In chapters 5 and 6 I will deal more thoroughly with this idea, especially as it relates to the concept of "modern-day" apostles. Sumrall's thoughts had not been fully developed about this concept at this time. However, he did hold that any further apostolic dimension to ministry would in no way replace the eyewitness role of the original twelve.

75. Synder, *Decoding the Church*, 91.

76. Frost and Hirsch, *Shape of Things to Come*, 170–72.

77. Sumrall, *New Wine Bottles*, 120.

78. Ibid., 116.

encouragement. Additionally, there were regional conferences throughout the year and a national conference for the entire fellowship once a year.

As time passed, sections of the articles were changed and the charter of LFCM became obsolete. Moreover, Sumrall began questioning some of his own views regarding extra-local government. Because of the regional structure of the fellowship, many pastors were relating to district overseers with whom they had no relationship. Frustrations followed. Church Foundational Network (CFN) soon began to form in Sumrall's mind. Its core conviction was that church government should be formed around relationships and not district or regional overseers. The next chapter will outline the historical beginnings of CFN, its reasons for being birth, and the governmental paradigm shift of Sumrall's thinking, especially concerning modern-day apostles.

5

Church Foundational Network

Transitioning from LFMC

BY 1995 LFMC WAS twenty years old. Sumrall had stepped down from overseeing the fellowship in 1990 and served only in an advisory capacity. However, by 1994 several of the presbytery members of LFMC began to express their concerns regarding their need for more mentoring and discipleship. At the national conference in 1995, Sumrall responded to their observations by speaking on church government. During the Friday night meeting, Sumrall covered three of his six points.[1] During the night, Sumrall reported that he could not sleep. He felt that the Lord was attempting to birth some new understanding about church government. In the early morning of the night, Sumrall believed that the Lord had spoken to him. "The pattern for governing the church is family; and families are led by fathers."[2]

Much of this new view on church government was in seed form when Sumrall wrote *New Wine Bottles*. For example, he stated that "one centralized organization under the same administration tends towards staleness and stagnation. But many flexible, 'extra-local organizations' (call them what you will) each one setting its own rules of relationships and whose apostolic leaders communicate and flow with each other, would promote stability, openness, unity of faith, and maturity in the kingdom of God."[3] When commenting on apostolic government he stated that "the apostles

---

1. Sumrall, *Apostolic Fathers and Their Families*, 2. His six points were (1) the privilege of being a coworker with Jesus in building his church; (2) the purpose of the church; (3) the priorities of the church; (4) the pattern of church government; (5) the principles that guide the church; and (6) the presence of the Holy Spirit in the church.

2. Ibid.

3. Sumrall, *New Wine Bottles*, 55.

establish the doctrinal and governmental foundation for local churches and ordain other elders to help oversee churches under their care. . . . Although this type government may appear to promote a centralized system where the whole body of Christ looks to one head, true apostolic government is not centralized. On the contrary, it allows for many apostles with separate administrations."[4] He added that apostolic government "is the theocratic system whereby the Lord oversees his body through delegated men."[5] Towards the end of the book, Sumrall stated strongly that it was his "firm conviction that until a minister is recognized as an apostle, he should minister under the supervision of an apostolic ministry which is proven and confirmed."[6] As the years followed, these incepted comments concerning church government was developing in Sumrall's thinking through the influence of several friends.

Instrumental Friends

Charles Simpson's friendship with Sumrall played a significant role in his developing thoughts on church government. From 1964 onward, Sumrall and Simpson prayed together regularly—almost weekly. They encouraged each other in a multitude of concerns, including authority issues, financial issues, areas of outside criticism, and troublemakers in the local church. They separated friendship from 1974 to 1985 because of Simpson's involvement in the Shepherding Movement. However, after their reconciliation in 1986 Simpson and Sumrall played golf together regularly. During this time Sumrall began to express some of his concerns for LFMC. After pondering Sumrall's apprehensions, Simpson maintained that LFMC had started treating Sumrall as a figurehead and that its direction was towards building the organization of LFMC. The result was that Sumrall was consulted less and less. During their golf games this became the primary issue about which Sumrall questioned Simpson. Simpson suggested a more "organic" approach to church government that focused more on relationships instead of the geographical leadership of a presbytery. From his time with Simpson, Sumrall's view on the need for a decentralized government began to solidify.[7]

---

4. Ibid., 62.
5. Ibid., 61–62.
6. Ibid., 135.
7. Simpson, interview with author, March 9, 2012.

L. A. Joiner's relationship with Sumrall was additionally paramount on his thinking concerning church government. In 1974 Joiner, who had just left the Navy, was looking for a place to be trained for the ministry. From his search he discovered Sumrall's school, Liberty Bible College. In the latter part of 1974 Joiner and his wife, Teresa, drove to Pensacola to hear Sumrall preach and visit the campus of Liberty. In the end, Joiner decided against attending Liberty. In the years that followed, Joiner would hear Sumrall preach and teach at the church where he was on staff in Waycross, Georgia. Through the years, Joiner's friendship with Sumrall would deepen. During one of Sumrall's visits, he preached on the fivefold ministry and its relevance for church government. From Sumrall's teaching, Joiner understood the fivefold ministry as a plurality of leaders who govern the local church. At that time, Joiner did not see this fivefold paradigm working within the church.[8]

In 1980 A. S. Worley, a missionary friend of Joiner's, encouraged him to join a group of godly men for accountability and encouragement. From his advice, Joiner asked Sumrall to be his pastor and mentor. As a result, Joiner was ordained by LFMC in the latter part of 1980.[9]

In 1990 Joiner resigned from New Covenant Church of Valdosta, Georgia, and moved to Houston, Texas, to plant a new church. The presbytery of LFMC asked Joiner to become the district overseer for Texas and Oklahoma. Joiner agreed, but soon became extremely uncomfortable with his new position within LFMC. Back in Georgia, his association with pastors and ministers were grounded in years of friendship, hence he had strong relationships with them. These personal connections were both rich and real due to the time in developing them. Joiner stated, "They were like sons to me."[10] Over time, Joiner became dissatisfied with LFMC's governmental structure. He concluded that leadership based upon appointments to a position instead of relationships was too political for him.[11]

From Joiner's point of view, a pastor is someone the individual should choose and not be assigned. This conviction grew to the point where Joiner drove from Texas to Pensacola, Florida, where he informed Sumrall that he did not desire to be in leadership with LFMC. Joiner maintained that a church government should be linked to the individual who birthed it.

8. Joiner, interview with author, December 11, 2012.
9. Ibid.
10. Ibid.
11. Ibid.

Apostles, whom Joiner considered "fathers," should be the key to church government. If the church moves from being governed apostolically to being governed by an administrator, then one has just formed a denomination. Joiner felt that only an apostle could truly advance the vision of the local church.[12]

After receiving Simpson's and Joiner's views on church government, Sumrall decided to bring a change to LFMC's governmental structure. He concluded that the best approach to this change would be for Joiner to share his views with the presbytery of LFMC. Joiner did so at their annual winter LFMC national conference in January 1995.[13] He said that what was needed was an apostolic government based upon a fivefold ministerial oversight through which people were governed relationally instead of regionally. The presbytery of LFMC asked Sumrall what was his opinion of Joiner's position. To their surprise, Sumrall stated that he was going to invest the rest of his life towards developing apostolic government in the local churches. By this time, however, Sumrall was not a member of the executive presbytery, so he asked their permission to lead LFMC again, and over time he would bring these governmental changes. The presbytery agreed, but by the next day they had changed their minds and said they did not desire this new form of government.[14] They understood that leadership would be defined by one's function as a fivefold minister and not by seniority,[15] and they did not agree with Sumrall's position of tithing to the apostle.[16]

Beginning Church Foundational Network

Sumrall knew that after twenty years of operating under a centralized form of government, it would be difficult for a maintenance oriented group of

12. Ibid.

13. Kelly, interview with author, May 12, 2012.

14. Many within the leadership structure of LFMC were afraid they would lose their position of leadership in the new governmental structure.

15. Joiner, interview with the author, December 11, 2012. One of Joiner's major concerns was the pastors who were relating to him as their pastor. LFMC policy was that when anyone joined LFMC, the churches under that individual must join LFMC as well. Joiner did not agree with this policy.

16. Ibid. It should be noted that these funds do not go directly to the individual (the apostle). Within CFN, each network is set up as a not-for-profit organization. The funds go to the organization, and the board of counselors sets the apostle's salary and is responsible for proper accounting procedures.

men to embrace a need to decentralize its leadership. Resistance grew week by week. The strongest resistance came when Sumrall stated that for the new government to function the fellowship's presbytery would need to be dissolved. The attitude of the LFMC's presbytery, according to Sumrall, was "if it's not broke, don't fix it."[17] Sumrall was convinced that this new government was the Lord's direction—where apostolic ministers could function as fathers of ministers who were related to them as their spiritual sons and daughters. In April of 1995 Sumrall resigned from LFMC to birth a network of ministerial families. Twenty-one ministers of LFMC joined Sumrall in this new governmental endeavor. The great majority from LFMC, approximately three hundred, remained with the fellowship.[18]

Sumrall's main objective for CFN was to decentralize ministerial accountability by placing authority to ordain and oversee ministers in the hands of their spiritual fathers and their councils. Apostolic fathers and their ministerial cells were authorized to ordain and license ministers within their cells. Afterwards, each ordained minister could apply to be a part of CFN through their various cells. Howbeit, the majority of their spiritual oversight would be with their spiritual father and his council.[19]

By the end of 1995, over one hundred ministers had connected with Sumrall and his new network. By 2003 the network had over twenty-two apostolic fathers who had their own cells, which had over six hundred ministers. All twenty-two leaders adopted Sumrall as their spiritual father and asked for input into their lives. At first, the thought was to call these structures "tribes," patterned after Moses' Old Testament model. But in the end the leaders concluded that it would not be accepted.[20]

Sumrall chose three ministers who were present at their first meeting to help him to work out the details of the new network, to help decide on a name for it, and to help form the charter for the overall vision for the network. These men included Jack Hollis, apostle of Associated Ministries of Marianna, Florida, and senior pastor of Christian Center Church; Marc Limbaugh, senior pastor of Christ Fellowship of Carrollton, Georgia; and L. A. Joiner, apostle of Christian Alliance of Ministers of Valdosta, Georgia, and senior pastor of New Covenant Church. Sumrall suggested that the network be patterned after the teaching points of Charles Simpson's material

17. Sumrall, *Apostolic Fathers*, 5.
18. Ibid., 5–7.
19. Ibid., 7–9.
20. Kelly, interview with author, May 12, 2012.

on vision, which he delivered to LFMC in one of their annual conferences. These included: (1) base your vision on a call from God; (2) accurately assess your character and gifts; (3) adopt a vision in which all participants can delight; (4) have the ability to attract people to the vision; and (5) form a strategy to improvise the vision. Using these criteria, Sumrall met with the leaders to finalize the charter. It was Lee Short, senior pastor of Family Life Center of Houston, Texas, and apostle of Lee Short Ministries (a missionary organization), who suggested the name Church Foundational Network. Additionally, they agreed that the ministerial groups would be called "ministerial cells."[21]

Their essential strategy was to form a non-centralized network that was based on relationships rather than on an organizational structure. Hence, the ministerial cells would not necessarily be geographical. They concluded that as long as a spiritual father could relate and communicate with his sons and daughters, they could be located in another city, state, or even a foreign country.[22] Moreover, rather than a spiritual father (i.e., apostle) seeking out sons or daughters, they would explore and adopt a spiritual father and ask them to be responsible for their oversight. If an apostolic father accepted them, then they connected to him and became part of his ministerial cell.[23]

Implementation

Sumrall's vision advanced a decentralized form of governmental structure as well as recognizing apostolic men. He firmly maintained that the pattern of church government was family, and families have spiritual fathers who give oversight to their sons and daughters. Not everyone of the primary group was ordained as an apostle. Time was given for each to give evidence of an anointing to function as apostles. The ones who were not ordained as apostles were approved as apostolic fathers who cared for those who related to them as sons and daughters.[24] Thereby one could be an apostolic father but not be recognized as an apostle.

Within CFN the ordination of these leaders required an accurate assessment of their gifts and character. Sumrall emphasized the need to walk

21. Sumrall, *Apostolic Fathers*, 9–14.
22. Ibid., 14.
23. Ibid., 15.
24. Ibid., 10.

circumspectly in identifying the fivefold ministry gifts within CFN. The point was to underscore one's function as a minister, not simply the title. Moreover, each ministerial cell had the final determination in identifying each minister's gift within their cell and could ordain them. Also, each cell formed its own policies and determined its own goals and vision within the broad boundaries of CFN.[25]

Sumrall confessed that CFN had the potential of being misunderstood. He intuitively knew that some would misinterpret CFN by accusing the network of controlling people. Others would disagree with the idea of present-day apostles in the church. However, he pointed out that the first apostles of the church at Jerusalem also faced scorn and ridicule. The gift of apostle was completely new to Israel at that time.[26] Bill Click, who had embraced the modern day apostolic paradigm, agreed. He stated:

> apostolic authority was released by Jesus to insure that His authority to advance the Kingdom would be properly identified, received and used. But the idea of an "apostle" was totally new to Israel. The only secular equivalent was with the Greek shipping fleets of the day, whose Captain's were sometimes given the title "apostle" to describe their authority as ambassadors representing those who had sent them. Therefore, this term and its implications were certainly foreign to the disciples.[27]

Sumrall's warnings proved true. Some misjudged the vision of CFN. The leadership of CFN decided not to answer their critics and kept their focus on the vision. Time would decide if they had heard from the Lord correctly.[28]

Sumrall's overall premise for his views concerning apostolic government had several foundational positions. First, the Holy Spirit is the chief administrator of the church. Sumrall taught that the first-century church was well trained, but knew they had a great need for the Holy Spirit to continue to guide them. He taught that without the Holy Spirit there would be no power, no divine guidance, no divine order in church government, nor any true freedom. The Spirit was the qualifier for raising up leaders, and without him the church would become nothing more than another human-made organization with human-directed programs and religious

---

25. Ibid., 12.
26. Ibid., 13.
27. Click, "Fully Foundational Church," para. 9.
28. Sumrall, *Apostolic Fathers*, 13.

formality. He stated that "we have counted on organization, personalities, and man's wisdom to promote the Kingdom of God. We must realize the answer is in honoring the Holy Spirit and seeking His way and not man's methods."[29] For Sumrall, the Spirit was and is the vicar of the church. Hence, all directions of the church must be subject to the will and direction of the Spirit. The government of the Spirit-led church was supernatural as the Spirit alone revealed the mind of the Lord. Sumrall understood that the Spirit's mind would be revealed through the fivefold ministers.[30]

Another concern for Sumrall was the need for balance. Sumrall's emphasis on theological equity came from his differences with Simpson's view of the Shepherding Movement. Sumrall believed that, since the days of Martin Luther, the church moved between two extremes: from excesses of individual freedom to an exaggerated position on submission and authority. He held that "too much stress on individual freedom breeds anarchy while strong teachings on governmental structure foster sectarianism and too much dependency on man."[31] What was needed was a balance between these two extremes. Sumrall posited the following:

> I am first of all responsible to the Lord God who only is sovereign. He speaks to me through His infallible, unchangeable Word. No man has any authority to violate God's authority over me stated in His Word or in my conscience. Also, if I am to obey the Lord and be subject to Him, then I must be submissive to authorities mentioned in the Word of God as being over me in the Lord.... I am an individual, but I must not be an individualist. According to the Word of God, I have been baptized by the Holy Spirit into the Body of Christ. I am not an isolated Christian but a member of the Lord's Body.[32]

Church government was vital for Sumrall, but it must be administered through the Spirit in balance with the Scriptures.

CFN and Denominational Modalities

The bottom line for Sumrall and CFN was how and by whom God governs his church. In his quest to understand godly government, he examined

29. Sumrall, *Practical Church Government*, 34.
30. Ibid., 33–36.
31. Ibid., 37.
32. Ibid., 39.

several forms of church government. Sumrall saw the episcopal form of church government as a centralized governmental structure. Bishops were elected to oversee a designated area that included several churches.[33] The simplest form of episcopal government was found in the Methodist Church, which has only one level of bishops. A more developed governmental structure was found in the Anglican or Episcopal Churches, while the Roman Catholic Church had the most complex system of hierarchy. Inherent in the episcopal structure was the idea of different levels of ministry or difference degrees of ordination.[34] However, the bishop was the key to the functioning of church government. Some would say that the episcopacy was the very essence of the church, and the church could not exist without it.[35] Hence, the power of the bishop was considerable, if not absolute.[36]

There were several arguments in supporting the episcopal form of government. It began with the declaration that Christ was the founder of the church.[37] As such, he provided the authoritative governing structure for the church. He sent forth his apostles in his kingdom authority (Matt 28:18). The apostles were the only officers Jesus appointed, and it could be concluded that they were the only New Testament persons with the right to exercise ecclesiastical oversight and authority.[38] However, they did delegate some of their authority to others, for example Timothy and Titus. Evidently the apostles also appointed elders and rulers in the local church (Acts 14:23) and ordained them. The next supporting position would be the function of James within the church of Jerusalem. His authority was similar to those held by later bishops and was the precedent for the episcopal system.[39] Finally, there was a historical argument for a direct line of succession from the apostles to modern-day bishops. Through the ordination process the authority of the apostles had been passed down to today's bishops.[40]

There were some notable objections to the episcopal form of church government. For Sumrall, the system was too formalized. It tended to

---

33. Ibid., 41.
34. Morris, "Church, Nature and Government of (Episcopalian View)," 2:483.
35. Hebert, *Form of the Church*, 109–23.
36. See Moede, *Office of Bishop in Methodism*. Throughout the history of the Methodist Church, for example, the amount of power granted to the bishops has varied.
37. Gratsch, "Development of Ecclesiology," 157–60.
38. Farrer, "Ministry in the New Testament," 131.
39. Ibid., 181.
40. Ott, *Fundamentals of Catholic Dogma*, 282–85.

emphasis the office rather than the person who held it. In the New Testament, authority was given only to those who were spiritually qualified and sound in doctrine. What a person was, did, believed, and taught were far more important than any position held. A man should not be accepted to an office in the church simply because he said that he belonged in a particular office. But he should be recognized by certain scriptural qualifications and by the fruit of his life.[41] The latter was to be determined by the former, not the former by the latter.[42] Also, exception could be taken to the theory of apostolic succession. There was no description in the Scriptures of any highly developed government. Additionally there was no report or command to preserve or perpetuate a particular form of government. Moreover, there were minimum indications of any difference of authority between bishops and elders. For instance, Acts 6:6 revealed the apostles laying their hands on the seven at Jerusalem, while Timothy received his gift through the elders' hands (1 Tim 4:14). Lastly, the episcopal form of church government did not give consideration to Christ's lordship over the church. Paul was installed as an apostle without any mediator (see Gal 1:15–17). If Paul received his office directly from God, might not others as well? Paul's situation underscored the case that apostolic authority does not seem to rest upon previous apostolic influence.[43] Moreover, there were churches not of apostolic foundation, for example Colossae. But the Colossians seemed not to lack in ministry. Again, some early church orders, including the *Didache*, were congregational in outlook.[44] Nevertheless, the episcopacy was undoubtedly universal in church practice.

Another government structure was the Presbyterian government. Sumrall held that the Greek word πρεσβύτερος was mainly translated as "elder" in the New Testament.[45] The presbyterian system placed primary authority in a particular office, but there was less emphasis upon the individual office or officeholder and more upon the representative body that exercised that authority. This form of government tended to harken back to the Jewish synagogue. They held the office because of their age and experience. In the New Testament, the authority of Christ was exercised through the delegated believer who was appointed as an elder. The elders functioned on behalf

---

41. Sumrall, *Apostolic Fathers and Their Families*, 40–41.
42. Hubert, *Form of the Church*, 110.
43. Morris, "Church Government," 126–27.
44. Ibid., 239.
45. Sumrall, *Practical Church Government*, 42.

of believers within the local body of Christ. It was at this level that elders discharged their divine authority within the church.[46] Within the Presbyterian Church in America, there are many levels of authority, from the local church up to the General Assembly. Decisions are made by the governing body at each level. However, these decisions were subject to review and revision by the next higher level. The point would be to interpret and apply the explicit teachings of the Lord, especially as these related to the church.[47]

The presbyterian system differed from the episcopal in that there was only one level of ministers. No higher levels, such as bishop, existed. Others objected to this form of government because it was rooted in a hierarchy of governing bodies with little support from Scripture.[48] This would be Sumrall's main objection. Additionally, much time was required to accomplish or to decide on a course of action. Decisions got bottled up in various committees.

The last form of government to which Sumrall objected was congregational government. This form of government allowed every member in the local body to vote on the affairs of the church. Business meetings were conducted regularly to determine the direction of the church. Ministers were elected or dismissed by majority vote of the congregation, and church officers were elected by the voting members of the church. Sumrall began his early ministry with this type of government.[49]

The two main concepts to the congregational scheme were autonomy and democracy. Each local congregation was independent and self-governing. No external power could dictate the course of action to the local church. A democratic government allowed every member to have a voice in the affairs of the church, regardless of their spiritual maturity. Hence authority was not the prerogative of a lone individual or a set group of leaders. Neither a monarchical nor an oligarchical structure could take the place of the individual. The main denominations that practice this form of government are Baptists, Congregationalists, and Lutherans (Lutherans also have bishops).[50]

With the congregational form of government, much was made concerning the priesthood of the believer. Many who held this position felt that

---

46. Presbyterian Church (U.S.A.) General Assembly, *Book of Order*, 39.01–39.04.
47. Erickson, *Christian Theology*, 1076.
48. Pieper, *Christian Dogmatics*, 3:421.
49. Sumrall, *Practical Church Government*, 42.
50. Pieper, *Christian Dogmatics*, 475.

the priesthood of the believer would be surrendered if bishops or elders were given the decision-making prerogative. They reminded others that Paul taught that each member or part of the body had a valuable contribution to make to the welfare of the church.[51]

Historically, congregationalism was a system from the Reformation era. Some from the Reformed perspective concretely rejected the idea of a state church and saw believers forming a "gathered church," those who heard the call of Christ and obeyed. Robert Browne, an Englishman, published a famous treatise in 1582 entitled "Reformation Without Tarrying for Any." In it he confirmed the idea of the gathered church, its independence of bishops and magistrates, and its authority to ordain its ministers. Forced from England because of his beliefs, he moved to Holland. It was from Leiden that the pilgrim fathers sailed to America in 1620 and established congregationalism in the new world. It became a part of the American religious culture.[52]

Those who were elected to represent the church did not exercise their powers independently of or contrary to the wishes of the people. Hence, within the congregational form of government there was only one level of clergy. Bishop, elder, and pastor were believed to be different names for the same office. The only other office was the lay office of deacon.[53]

There were several objections to the congregational form of church government. First, the congregational scheme seemed to disregard the biblical evidence for apostolic authority. Paul did appoint elders and instructed Titus to do the same (see Acts 14:23 and Tit 1:5). On many occasions when Paul wrote to the churches, he did not simply offer advice; he virtually commanded them to heed what he had written.[54] Next, Scripture bore out a separation between the offices of bishop, elder, and deacon early in church history. To dismiss this assumption would require one to depart from New Testament foundations concerning authority within the church. Lastly, John's letters to the seven churches in the book of Revelation were addressed to the "angel" or "messenger" of the respective congregations. Most understand this to be the ruling elder for each congregation.

---

51. McNutt, *Polity and Practice in Baptist Churches*, 21–26.

52. Morris, "Church Government," 240.

53. Strong, *Systematic Theology*, 914–15.

54. Sumrall, *Apostolic Fathers and Their Families*, 27–29. Also see Harris, "Church, Nature and Government of (Presbyterian View)," 2:490.

Apostolic Government of CFN

Sumrall rejected the above-mentioned forms of government. He was convinced that the best government for the present-day church was a theocracy. He pointed out that this New Testament form of government was first patterned in the Old Testament. Citing various scriptures, Sumrall mentioned that the children of Israel were led out of Egypt through the governmental structure of a theocracy. For him, "Moses was chosen by God as the first 'apostle' of His 'church in the wildness' (Exodus 2:3; Acts 7:38)."[55] Israel's failures and victories depended upon their compliance or dismissal of God's appointed leadership.

While Sumrall admitted that denominations have served a good purpose, he believed that their negatives far out weighted their positives. First, Sumrall maintained that promotions in denominations were based upon seniority. In so doing, they oftentimes promoted people beyond their giftedness. Many denominations were led by administrators and not visionaries. Next, many denominations owned the local church properties and, as such, could control the internal affairs of the local church. Lastly, over time the denominational structure tended to become a wineskin that was rigid, and the people become bound by rote traditions.[56]

From the New Testament, Sumrall believed that the church had become God's nation to advance his kingdom.[57] Where Jesus Christ ruled his church through delegated authority, there was pure theocracy. First mentioned in Josephus,[58] theocracy means the rule of God (θεο = God; κρατειν = to rule). However, the idea goes back to the Old Testament.[59] The law of the kings was recognized as the ultimate control of God.[60] As such, David's rule was the most theocratic kingship in scripture.

As coined by Josephus, the term's meaning was not just political in nature. It included every sphere and relationship in life, as governed in the Old Testament through a contemporaneous and continuing special

---

55. Sumrall, *Apostolic Fathers and Their Families*, 20.

56. Ibid., 24–25.

57. Sumrall, *New Wine Bottles*, 29–30. He supported this premise with Scripture: Matt 21:43 and 1 Pet 2:9.

58. Josephus, *Complete Works*, 630.

59. Sumrall, *Practical Church Government*, 31. He cited Exod 19:4–9.

60. Ibid.

revelation of God. God used human agencies to enable Israel to carry out his will. These included kings, prophets, priests, and Levites.[61]

From the example of Scripture, Sumrall advanced several foundational principles for apostolic government. First, he stated that organization was necessary for order and peace. While the Scriptures revealed various templates for the church (i.e., a body, a nation, a temple, a family, an army, and a flock), each one needed organization. Citing various examples from Scripture, Sumrall taught that the members of the body of Christ were positioned to function in an orderly fashion.[62] From these passages, he concluded that the church was not described as a jellyfish without structure, but rather as a human body where each member could operate properly because of organization. He underscored the elasticity of the wineskin (Luke 5:38–39), which revealed the essence of church government—organized flexibility.[63]

Second, Sumrall understood that governmental structure for God's people was built around need. The biblical examples for him were the Jethro principle of Exodus 18 and the raising up of the seventy elders of Numbers 11. He deduced that God saw a need for a presbytery of elders, who were chosen from the whole body of elders, to stand with Moses so as to determine God's direction for all the tribes and their leaders.[64]

Third, Sumrall said that after the church was established, a plurality of elders was needed in every local congregation. An elder, for Sumrall, was a spiritually mature male believer who was chosen to help oversee a local church. It was only after elders were appointed that the gathered believers were called the church (Acts 14:20–23). He pointed out that the fivefold office gifts of Eph 4:11–12 were elders, but not all elders were among those five offices.[65]

Last, Sumrall maintained that the plurality of elders needed a leader. Moreover, Sumrall insisted that the elders were not given equal responsibilities or authority. Some were rulers over thousands, some ruled over hundreds, some ruled over fifties, and some ruled over ten (see Exod 18:25). Sumrall was greatly influenced by Oswald J. Smith's view that God chose a man to lead his people.

---

61. Wyngaarden, "Theocracy," 1083.
62. Sumrall, *Practical Church Government*, 42–44. He cited 1 Cor 12:12, 15–23, 28.
63. Ibid., 43–44.
64. Ibid., 44–46.
65. Ibid., 47.

> God's plan is that his flock should be led by a shepherd, not run by a board.... The Holy Spirit appoints men.... The Bible knows no other plan. All down the centuries it has been the same. When God wanted something done he chose a man, equipped and fitted him for the task, placed him at the head of his people and told them to follow and obey.
>
> God . . . wants a deliverer and he takes Moses. He might have gone to the elders of Israel and selected a board. He did not. His call is to one man. To him he gives the vision, and Moses becomes God's representative, the great leader of his people.[66]

Every presbytery of elders needed a leader, if it was going to be biblical. Elders were needed to help care for the flock. But they were not equal in function. While Sumrall never embraced an autocratic church government, his firm conviction was for the church to be led by a plurality of elders who served under a leader.[67] So strong was this paradigm for him that he stated he would rather have a church with congregational government where the majority ruled than be under the dominion of strong-willed elders who would never allow him to lead and initiate ministry as the Lord would lead him.[68]

Equally strong was his conviction that church government should be a team effort. Any godly leader would desire counsel and advice from the church elders, and he should listen to their suggestions and even objections. If not, then he would not be a team player. He maintained that every local church should have a plurality of leadership, and that plurality best functions with a responsible man of God to whom the others would look to for oversight and guidance. Within CFN, this leader would be the modern-day apostle.

Additionally, Sumrall understood the pattern of church government for today to be family, where modern-day apostles would be spiritual fathers just as natural families have fathers. It was his firm conviction that all over the world sons and daughters were crying out for recognition from their spiritual fathers. The Spirit of God was touching certain men and inspiring them to raise up their sons and daughters, who in turn would raise up their own spiritual family. The church, for Sumrall, was shifting to prepare for this apostolic movement and to become an apostolic people.

---

66. Smith, *God's Plan for Leadership*, 3–4.

67. See Sumrall, *Practical Church Government*, 51. During his earlier years, Sumrall believed this leader to be the senior pastor, but with the passing of time he came to believe the senior leader was the modern-day apostle.

68. Ibid., 54.

These believers would be under a covering of an apostolic team led by a modern-day apostle. This new wineskin of church government had been established for the harvest. Sumrall believed that many new converts would be coming in from cultures that would not fit into the present-day institutional church.[69]

Summary

As early as 1975, Sumrall was pondering on the need for a newer form of church government that would allow the church to be more organic. For that to be a reality, church government needed to be flexible through emphasizing relationships. Over time and with the help of his trusted friends, Sumrall embraced a fivefold paradigm for church government. The center of this new structure was the recognition of modern-day apostles as fathers who would care for and nourish the leaders and their body of believers under their oversight.

This new door of governmental structure was considered by Sumrall as part of the restoration work of the Holy Spirit. Over time, however, questions began to surface for CFN and other apostolic networks. What was an apostle? How does an apostle function in the church? What were the main characteristics of these networks? These, and others, are the questions to be discussed in the next chapter.

---

69. Sumrall, *Apostolic Fathers and Their Families*, iv-vi.

6

Understanding the Modern-Day Apostle

PENTECOSTALS HAVE FREQUENTLY BEEN called "restorationists" because of their focus to call the church catholic back to the apostolic faith of the New Testament. This movement has grown throughout the years to embrace approximately six hundred million people around the world.[1] As such, it's the second largest group of Christians on the planet.[2]

The small church of the Azusa Street revival of 1906 was named the "Apostolic Faith Mission," and its periodical was called *Apostolic Faith*. At that time, Pentecostals did not believe in apostolic succession. The Roman Catholic doctrine that the bishops of their church were in direct succession of the original apostles was fully entrenched within Western thought. But Pentecostals understood the necessity that each believer needed to be filled with first-century apostolic power and wisdom in order to evangelize the world.

Though the name "apostolic" usually occurred in the names of their churches or storefront missions, sporadically their leaders would be called "apostles." Over time, attention has been focused on the inclusion of apostles in the fivefold ministry of Eph 4:11f. At issue was the question of cessation. If one believed that the gifts of the Holy Spirit were still in operation, then how could one maintain the position that the gift of the apostle was not recognized for today?

After World War II, the New Order of the Latter Rain movement challenged the weakening spirituality of the Pentecostal movement due to the increasing bureaucratization of their fellowships. Springing out of a revival in North Battleford, Saskatchewan, in 1948, the New Order of the

---

1. Barrett, Johnson, and Crossings, "Missiometrics 2005," 29.
2. Ibid. According to Barret, the Roman Catholic Church is the first.

Understanding the Modern-Day Apostle

Latter Rain taught that God was pouring out the "latter rain" and restoring apostles and prophets to the local church leadership.[3] Most Pentecostals quickly renounced the New Order over doctrinal differences. Consequently, it gradually lost influence and credibility.

Over fifty years later, the matter of the restoration of apostles to the church resurfaced. Perennially embraced by numerous independent Pentecostal and charismatic churches, restoration received a prominent endorsement during the National Symposium on the Post-Denominational Church, which was convened by C. Peter Wagner at Fuller Seminary, May 21–23, 1996. Wagner called this restoration movement the New Apostolic Reformation. He maintained that we were witnessing a reinventing of world Christianity.[4]

Wagner posited several characteristics for this renewal movement. The first one had to do with leadership. The main difference was the amount of authority delegated by the Spirit to the individual. He believed that the apostolic movement brought "a transition from bureaucratic authority to personal authority, from legal structure to relational structure, from control to coordination and from rational leadership to charismatic leadership. This all manifested itself on two levels: the local level and the translocal levels."[5] The second major emphasis for Wagner was leadership training. The leaders were dedicated to the equipping and releasing of the individual believer to do the work of the ministry. Members were taught to discover the spiritual gifts God had given them and to minister those gifts to others, both inside and outside the church. The third assertion had to do with their ministry paradigm. Traditional churches were "heritage driven" and began with their current situation and looked to the past. Apostolic churches were "vision driven" and began with their present situation and looked toward the future. The fourth characteristic had to do with its worship style. Contemporary worship was the style for apostolic churches. Many older hymns were rewritten with a more modern flare to them. Other characteristics included prayer forms, finances, new outreaches, and a sincere openness to the work of the Holy Spirit. It was the supernatural power of the Spirit's presence that opened the way for applying truth and not vice versa.[6]

---

3. McGee, *People of the Spirit*, 333–37.
4. Wagner, "New Apostolic Reformation," 25.
5. Ibid., 19–20.
6. Ibid., 19–25. For other insights to the various distinctives concerning the apostolic reformation movement see Miller, *Reinventing American Protestantism*, and Towns,

While one may agree or disagree with Wagner's assessment of the new apostolic movement, Wagner was so sure of his convictions that in 1999 he organized a network of apostolic ministers/ministries by birthing an apostolic covering named the International Coalition of Apostles. Sumrall joined Wagner's network for the purpose of associating with other leaders of like vision and passion.[7] As such, it is helpful to investigate Sumrall's understanding of the role of the modern-day apostle.

Defining an Apostle

In order to move into this new position, Sumrall believed that there would be plenty of challenges to the traditional views of church government. Restoration tended to address one's theology and required a change to one's way of thinking. The fivefold gifts of Eph 4:11f. gave to the apostolic restoration movement a new way of understanding how churches were planted and built. The Book of Acts underscored the fact that churches were planted by apostles and apostolic teams, not pastors. Just how, then, does one define a modern-day apostle?

At first, the word *apostello* was not a Christian term. It was used within the Greek culture to define leaders who were sent to colonize areas. As such, they had authority and control over the expedition, usually sailing vessels that transported both people and cargo to the expanded region.[8] Hence, an apostle was seen as an ambassador with authority because he represented the authority of the sender. The implications from this secular use of the word had important understanding for the modern term "apostle." It provided a framework for understanding how apostles operated in the church and in the larger realm of the kingdom of God. This can be seen in the definition of several leaders and authors who have embraced the new apostolic movement.

C. Peter Wagner defined the character of the modern-day apostle as "the special ability that God gives to certain members of the Body of Christ to assume and exercise general leadership over a number of churches with an extraordinary authority in spiritual matters that is spontaneously recognized and appreciated by those churches."[9] In his definition, what was im-

---

"Understanding the Cycles of Church Renewal."

7. Simpson, email message to author, March 26, 2013.
8. Moulton and Milligan, *Vocabulary of the Greek New Testament*, 69–70.
9. Wagner, *Your Spiritual Gifts Can Help Your Church Grow*, 231.

portant for Wagner was "authority." It was essential for his understanding because it avoided confusing apostle with the gift of a missionary. For Wagner, "the gift of missionary is the special ability that God gives to certain members of the Body of Christ to minister whatever other spiritual gifts they have in a second culture."[10] He used Paul and Peter to make his point. Paul was an apostle and had the gift of being a missionary. He was called to the uncircumcision, the Gentiles. Thereby, his gift was one of authority over the church and was also cross-cultural. Peter's gift was only to the Jews; as a Jew, he was not crossing cultures to minister to them.[11] Hence, Peter's gift was one of an apostle only.

Another leader, Bill Hamon, founder of Christian International Ministries, believed that the term "apostle" carried the meaning of one being sent forth for a specific purpose or commissioned to accomplish a specific task or ministry. As such, Hamon maintained that apostles were an extension of Jesus Christ, who was the great apostle. He added that the root meaning of the word implied "one sent as representative of another," and thereby had the power and authority of the representative who sent him. They were much like an ambassador who represented a country.[12] He stated his formal definition as the following:

> One of the fivefold ministries of Ephesians 4:11. The Apostle is a foundation-laying ministry (Eph. 2:20) that we see in the New Testament establishing new churches (Paul's missionary journeys), correcting error by establishing proper order and structure (First Epistle to the Corinthians), and acting as an oversight ministry that fathers other ministries (1 Cor. 4:15; 2 Cor. 11:28). The New Testament Apostle has a revelatory anointing (Eph. 3:5). Some major characteristics are great patience and manifestations of signs, wonders, and miracles. We will know more and see greater manifestations concerning the apostle during the peak of the Apostolic Movement.[13]

In short, Hamon saw the apostle as a person who had been divinely gifted with the nature and ability of Christ the apostle.[14]

---

10. Ibid., 233.
11. Wagner, *Churchquake*, 105–6.
12. Hamon, *Apostles, Prophets, and the Coming Moves of God*, 1, 28,124.
13. Ibid., 279.
14. Ibid., 55.

David Cannistraci's book *The Gift of Apostle* also defined "apostle" in naval terms. For him, the title was used of men who were naval officers or merchant mariners, who were responsible for the entire fleet of ships. For today's understanding, Cannistraci underscored the relationship of those who were sent to the sender. They represented the one by whom they were sent. As such, they faithfully transmitted or reflected the intentions of the sender. They were charged with dealing with changeable circumstances or conditions and handling difficult situations so as to please their superiors. Apostle meant "messenger" or "one that is sent with orders." They were delegates on a clear mission who were sent to be representative of their commanders and to establish their orders.[15] Apostles were "called and sent by Christ to have spiritual authority, character, gifts and abilities to successfully reach and establish people in Kingdom truth and order, especially through founding and overseeing local churches."[16] They were tasked with a mission of equipping an apostolic people, who would help build apostolic churches and create an apostolic movement.[17]

Alan Hirsch defined "apostle" and "apostolic" within a missional matrix. In commenting on Eph 4:11–12, Hirsch maintained that it revealed fundamental insights into Paul's ecclesiology. As such, it would be understood as a fundamental description—even a prescription—for the church of all ages. He saw this passage of Scripture not as an office gift for the church, but more in terms of function. Jesus' gracing of the church could not be institutionalized into an office. He flatly denied that to assert the ongoing validity of apostolic service and ministry was to suggest a reinstitution of the apostolic office of the original Twelve.[18]

Hirsch described apostolic leadership as bottom-up and highly relational. For far too long the church had been captivated by hierarchical, top-down conceptions of leadership, which had inadvertently blocked the power latent in the people of God. Apostolic ministry called for and developed the gifts and callings of all of God's people. It developed the capacities of the whole people of God based upon the dynamics of the gospel. Thereby, it involved empowerment.[19] Oftentimes dominant, charismatic leaders

---

15. Cannistraci, *Gift of Apostle*, 84–85.
16. Ibid., 29, 91.
17. Ibid., 29.
18. Frost and Hirsch, *Shape of Things to Come*, 166–69.
19. Hirsch, *Forgotten Ways*, 163–64.

can become one of the greatest deterrents for an organization moving from being good to becoming great.[20]

From these characteristics of an apostolic, Hirsch advanced both a generic and a biblical definition of the term. In the generic sense, apostles were those sent to pioneer something new. Reflected in the orders of creation, these would be teachers who turned around failing schools, people who started movements of sorts, or entrepreneurial business individuals.[21] Biblically, he defined an apostle as one who was "tasked with the overall vigor, as well as extension of Christianity as a whole, primarily through direct mission and church planting. As the name itself suggests, it is the quintessentially missional ministry, as 'sentness' (Latin *mission*) is written into it (*apostello*=sent one)."[22]

Sumrall's Understanding Concerning Apostles

By 1975 Sumrall was beginning to believe that the charismatic renewal was a restoration movement that aimed at restoring New Testament power and order to the church. This undertaking of the Spirit included the restoring of "fathers" to the church. The seed for this thought started in 1966. Sumrall was overseeing a building project of Liberty Church. He met a young boy of the ripe age of five. Stevie, who lived by the church property, would often follow him around the campus asking questions and boldly stating his opinion as Sumrall directed the development of the building process. Stevie had come from a troubled home and would often use "street language" in responding to Sumrall. Sumrall saw the opportunity for a strong hand in the boy's life as well as encouraging love. He recounted his conversation with Stevie that started his thinking concerning the restoration of "fathers" to the church.

> One day as he stood observing my work, his excited eyes watching every move I made with profound interest and his ears alert to all that I said to working on different projects, he asked: "Are you the daddy of this gang?"

---

20. Collins, *Good to Great*, 17–40. Great discussion on how a leader can advance or hinder an organization.

21. Hirsch credits this idea to Dowsett, "Recovering the Fivefold Ministry of the Local Church."

22. Hirsch and Catchim, *Permanent Revolution*, 8–9.

"Well, I guess you would say that I am the daddy of this gang."
I answered rather nonchalantly.

He quickly responded with: "Then why do they call you Brother Ken?"[23]

Sumrall tried to explain to the young boy the concept of the family of God. He encouraged the young boy to become a part of the family of God by accepting Jesus into his life. Stevie responded and prayed for Jesus to forgive his sins and come into his life. After praying, Sumrall remembered the following: "Then looking up with a sincere expression he asked me: 'Am I your brother now?' 'If you really meant it, Stevie, I am your brother and your spiritual daddy, too.'"[24] Soon after his encounter with him, Stevie moved away. But Sumrall began to see all the students who started coming to Liberty Bible College as a family, with himself as "the daddy of this gang."

It was this fatherhood paradigm that caused Sumrall to think about adjusting his views on church government. One such modification, which supplemented his growing understanding of the apostolic, was extra-local authorities. Sumrall believed that extra-local authorities extended beyond the local church. They were not independent and autonomous, with local elders or congregations acting sovereignly. But they were joined together by an administrator who was commissioned by the Holy Spirit to minister beyond a local church. To substantiate his position, he cited Peter and John's authority in Samaria (Acts 8:14), the sending forth of Paul and Barnabas by the Antioch elders (Acts 13:1–3), the sending forth of decrees to all the churches by the Jerusalem council (Acts 15:1–21), and Paul's authority over the churches he pioneered. He concluded that extra-local authorities were a biblical concept, and that these leaders embodied the fivefold ministry of Eph 4:11–12.[25]

At this time Sumrall was not necessarily opposed to a centralized governmental structure. When asked about setting up a sectarian denomination through this form of government, Sumrall stated that he believed church history pointed out that every move of God had a tendency to become exclusive, competitive, and overly organized. However, he confirmed that more permanent fruit came through organizing the believers than

---

23. Sumrall, *New Wine Bottles*, 17.
24. Ibid.
25. Ibid., 109–11.

through independent believers who refused to come together. For Sumrall, apostles were the key to substantiating the fruit of the charismatic renewal.[26]

At this time, Sumrall defined an apostle as "an envoy or one sent forth on a special mission."[27] He stated that the main difference between modern-day apostles and the twelve chosen by Jesus was in the mission and authority required by the one sending them. Jesus chose, trained, and sent the first twelve apostles to establish the believers in the "apostle's doctrine." They were eyewitnesses of Jesus' earthly ministry, death, and resurrection/ascension. They bridged the Old Testament and the New Testament and had the future ministry of judging the twelve tribes of Israel (Rev 21:14). However, Sumrall believed that the Holy Spirit was still sending forth apostles, just like the example of Paul and Barnabas in Acts 13. He pointed out that the Scriptures mentioned at lease twenty-six apostles in the New Testament. Howbeit, the major error that many made was to elevate all apostles to the ministry of the first twelve or Paul, which left no place for apostles who were sent by the Spirit. Nevertheless, Sumrall maintained that the traditional teaching of only twelve apostles in the New Testament must be discarded if one was to accept the Bible as inspired Scripture.[28] Interestingly Hippolytus of Rome, a third-century father of the church, gave the names and description of seventy apostles.[29] Throughout the late 1970s and 1980s Sumrall maintained the following definition of a modern-day apostle: "one sent as a messenger, the bearer of a commission, church planter, spiritual father of a congregation or fellowship, God's anointed leader of a fellowship."[30]

By the time Sumrall birthed CFN in 1995, his understanding of modern-day apostles shifted towards apostles being "spiritual fathers." He was convinced that the church was experiencing the fulfillment of the Elijah ministry. Citing Matt 17:10–12, the first Elijah was John the Baptist, who came to prepare the way for the Lord. The second Elijah, based upon Mal 4:5–6, would be those ministers who would bring in the last great harvest before the return of the Lord.

---

26. Ibid., 118–19.

27. Ibid., 127.

28. Ibid., 128–29.

29. Hippolytus, "Same Hippolytus on the Seventy Apostles," in *Ante-Nicene Fathers*, 5:255–56.

30. Sumrall, *New Wine Bottles*, 183.

He believed that the Lord was preparing the church for the greatest outpouring of the Holy Spirit in all of church history. He affirmed that God would accomplish this spiritual mandate through several issues. First, the Lord was placing a hunger in the hearts of people for spiritual awakening. Second, the Spirit was creating a desire in fathers to turn their hearts to their sons and daughters. Sumrall felt that this was true in natural families as well in spiritual families. Third, God was releasing an apostolic anointing on men and inspiring them to raise up ministerial sons and daughters. These spiritual kids would, in turn, raise up their own spiritual families. Fourth, the church was changing to accommodate this apostolic movement, and as such, would equip and train an apostolic people. Sumrall firmly believed that the word "apostle" would be widely recognized across the church world just like the words "pastor" and "evangelist" were. Last, new wineskins would be needed to allow this new apostolic movement to continue. He strongly believed that this new governmental structure would be family. Just like natural families, God's government would be spiritual fathers who would care for the flock. For Sumrall, these spiritual fathers would be apostles.[31]

Function of Apostles

Leaders of the Pentecostal outpouring of the early 1900s argued that the Holy Spirit was restoring the charismata to the church after many centuries of absence. The essence of its belief was that the work of the Holy Spirit in the life of the believer and the body of Christ was the same today as it was in the beginning era of the church. Their belief was that the Holy Spirit had not changed, and the manifestations of the Spirit that were current in the time of the first apostles should be expected today. Working from this paradigm, modern-day Pentecostals and charismatics applied this understanding to include the definition of Christian ministry. Thereby, if charismatic gifts were restored, then apostles, prophets, evangelists, pastors, and teachers were as well. Hence, the logic of restorationism, as Sumrall believed, was an all-or-nothing rationale. Restorationists would not argue for a partial renewing work of the Spirit. They advocated for everything that the Spirit gave and inspired. Since Pentecostals and charismatics argued for

---

31. Ibid., iii–vi.

the continuing functions of the gifts of the Spirit, it followed that the New Testament pattern for ministry would also be restored.[32]

Throughout the 1960s, as the charismatic movement was in full swing, talk of restoring apostles and prophets was limited. But by the 1970s the subject was again in circulation. Sumrall was influenced during this time by author John Noble. His books *Forgive Us Our Denominations* and *First Apostles Last Apostles* made a lasting impression on him, especially concerning the function of modern-day apostles. In the latter, Noble gave a summary of the history of the church, beginning with the first century and then regretting the gradual loss of its authority and power. He maintained that "every trace of unbelief concerning the appearance of apostles must be dealt with, so that we may watch and pray with faith for the men of God's appointment to come forth in power.... They will unite and release an army under God which will accomplish His purpose in these end-times."[33] Noble stated that after the first apostles died the wrong people filled their place. Bishops and elders replaced the role of apostle, and a central organization emerged when the pope displaced apostolic authority. While Catholicism invested too much authority in one man, Protestants made the opposite mistake of giving every individual the right to rule the church. Sumrall embraced Noble's position that God's intention was that there should be a plurality of leadership in mutual submission and that local elders would come into a relationship of trust with an apostolic ministry.[34] These apostles would build upon the foundation of Christ, the chief apostle. Moreover, the apostle was like a father and had the authority to appoint elders by choosing individuals from within the body of the fellowship to whom he related.[35]

Sumrall understood that the modern-day apostle had several functions. First, apostles were church planters and master builders. A key element for apostles was to plant and establish congregations on biblical foundations.[36] The pattern in the Book of Acts was straightforward for Sumrall. Apostles were sent to penetrate cities and establish local churches. By tracing the example of Paul's life, the pattern was clear. Apostles built churches—not

---

32. Kay, *Apostolic Networks in Britain*, 241. Also see Kay, *Pentecostals in Britain*.
33. Noble, *First Apostles, Last Apostles*, 25.
34. Sumrall, *Practical Church Government*, 48–53.
35. Ibid.
36. Sumrall, *New Wine Bottles*, 130. Also see Sumrall, *Apostolic Fathers*, 82.

the building of course, but congregations.[37] Second, apostles operated with great patience and oftentimes endured suffering. Sumrall considered this aspect of being an apostle extremely important. While it was not as exciting as birthing churches, it was important because it had to do with the individual's character.[38] Above all, an apostle remained persistent and true in times of opposition. David Cannistraci, another author who influenced Sumrall, quoted a fundamental statement given by Costa Deir, their mutual friend, concerning apostleship. He asserted, "You Americans are always looking for the outward marks of ministry in order to make a quick association with a title. But apostleship is first an internal quality. We easterners look at the character and the things inside an individual that define who he is."[39] For Sumrall, apostleship was a matter of character above any other single quality. Third, Sumrall asserted that signs and wonders would follow apostles. He quoted 2 Cor 12:12 as the biblical mandate for apostles. Without signs, Sumrall maintained that the church should question their calling. Additionally, God's people would witness more supernatural signs. Sumrall understood that there would be a maturing process. He stated that there would be "more and more of the power signs in developing apostles as this present restoration progresses, and as the apostles mature in their callings."[40] Fourth, Sumrall taught that modern-day apostles had a passion to care for the churches. He believed that "the office of the apostle is not one of superiority, as the father of a home is not superior to the rest of the family. He just works with a different responsibility and authority. Just as there are different ages, maturity levels, and methods of oversight in natural fathers, so there are in the spiritual realm."[41] His emphasis was not necessarily on the church in general but primarily on developing leaders who minister within the church. Sumrall believed that those with apostolic anointing and calling were visionaries and would blossom as pioneers and spiritual fathers when placed in a visionary arena. His calling was to provide such a place for developing apostles and prophets within the church.[42]

---

37. McBirnie, *Search for the Early Church*, 27–28.
38. Sumrall, *New Wine Bottles*, 131. Also see Sumrall, *Apostolic Fathers*, 82.
39. Cannistraci, *Apostles and the Emerging Apostolic Movement*, 107.
40. Sumrall, *Apostolic Fathers and Their Families*, 84.
41. Ibid., 85.
42. Ibid.

Modern Apostles' Greatest Function: Spiritual Fathers

Sumrall understood the greatest function of the modern-day apostle as being a "spiritual father." They had a God-given ability to gather other anointed men around them, thereby forming a team. These apostles did not strive for this position but were simply recognized as "father" by other men and women.[43] Their authority would be expressed in and through personal relationships rather than by virtue of their rank. Sumrall held that every minister needed to be in a small cell of ministers who were overseen by a spiritual father and his council.[44] He taught that the apostle and his council would impart wisdom and insight into the lives of ministers who related to him—especially young ministers. This fathering skill would be copiously taught and conveyed as the apostolic movement evolved. Others felt as Sumrall did. Frank Damazio lamented that "the world has thousands of erudite scholars, but the church is crying out for the ministry of spiritual fathers."[45] Fathers would take a powerful part in the process of directing and guiding their sons and daughters in their discipleship growth. Like natural fathers, their main aim would be to direct their disciples into productive paths.[46] Hence it would include instruction, adjustments, corrections, and discipline. Sumrall believed that if a minister was to get instruction, then he should also take correction. If all one desired was a teacher, then he did not want oversight but instruction only. He was firm in this conviction and staunchly declared on many occasions, "The Scripture refers to this kind of person—who does not want rebuke—as a spiritual bastard."[47]

Second, Sumrall understood fathers as encouragers. Few relationships could surpass the encouragement a father can give to their sons and daughters. For Sumrall, there was a major difference between being a mentor and being a spiritual father. A person can have several mentors but only one father. People don't just need empathy or sympathy; they need encouragers. Encouragement meant putting courage into people. One of the major responsibilities of a spiritual father was to motivate their sons and daughters

---

43. Sumrall, *New Wine Bottles*, 132.
44. Sumrall, *Apostolic Fathers and Their Families*, 59.
45. Damazio, *Making of a Leader*, 56.
46. The influence of Charles Simpson can easily be seen in many of Sumrall's views concerning "spiritual fathering."
47. Sumrall, *Apostolic Fathers and Their Families*, 60. Additionally, I have been in several meeting when Sumrall would make such a statement concerning the necessity for spiritual fathering.

to embrace their destiny in the kingdom of God.[48] Without this fatherly affection, apostles would become an overbearing and oppressive influence in the church.

Third, apostles, for Sumrall, were fathers who blessed and imparted. He held that the laying on of hands to bless and impart was a foundational doctrine of Scripture (Hebrews 6). He discerned this apostolic, fatherly function throughout the Bible. Consider the poignant stories of the prophets and patriarchs. For example, Jacob so coveted his father's blessing that he tricked the aging Isaac into giving it to him instead of Esau. Jacob would lay hands on his son Joseph's children and bless them. Apostolic fathers today were rediscovering the power involved in ministering to both their natural and spiritual sons and daughters. Moreover, the apostles who wrote the Scriptures were careful to open and close their letters by imparting a spiritual blessing to their readers. Sumrall stated the purpose of impartation and blessing was to not only ordain but to even call forth spiritual gifts. He believed "that fathers often impart courage, security, a sense of destiny and sometimes an anointing for a ministry by the laying on of their hands."[49]

In the end, Sumrall understood spiritual fathers as exercising their gift in two primary dimensions. First was their level of authority from a corporate perspective. The local churches for which Paul had apostolic oversight, for example, would have him as their spiritual father (see 1 Cor 4:15). At one point, Sumrall considered calling the various groups in CFN "tribes."[50] This was based upon the Old Testament tribes of the children of Israel. The entire exchange of authority, inheritances, relationships, and resources were all arranged according to families. Moreover, Abraham was the patriarch to a household of thousands whose faith speaks today. For Sumrall, the entire Old Testament narrative was built around the households and families of the lineage of Christ and God's dealings with these households. Likewise, the New Testament was filled with language that described spiritual tribes and households within the family of God. Paul described the body of Christ as the "household of faith" (Gal 6:10) and as the "household of God" (Eph 2:19). Thereby, modern-day apostles would govern corporately with the help of elders and pastors over the various tribes (which Sumrall later

---

48. Ibid., 59–62.

49. Ibid., 64.

50. Sumrall, *Practical Church Government*, 44–46; and *Apostolic Fathers and Their Families*, 7.

changed to ministerial cells). The conglomeration of all these various tribes made up the spiritual nation of the church.

The second dimension was in the realm of "begetting." The word itself speaks of causing to become, which is distinct from simply giving birth. From Scripture, fathers caused their sons and daughters to become something. It underscored the importance of the relationship between the apostle and his council and those who looked to them for counsel. Spiritual fathers would take an influential part in directing and guiding those who related to them. They would lead them into activities and attitudes that would prepare them for success. The Scriptures stated that fathers were to raise their children to a place of maturity and fruitfulness (Eph 6:4). Intrinsic to the meaning of begetting was to provide. For Sumrall, this meant to be responsible for their spiritual well-being and leaving a spiritual legacy.[51] The most valuable heritage a spiritual father could leave to their sons and daughters would be to impart their own spiritual drive and ability. As such, fathers carried the seed of the next generation in their lives. They begat and enlarged the kingdom of God through their ministries. For Sumrall, this ministry of spiritual fathers was essential to the life and vitality of the body of Christ, and was the primary reason apostles were so desperately needed for today.

Synthesizing Modern-Day Apostles

In order to comprehend and apply modern-day apostles and the apostolic movement, Sumrall understood that there would be much reframing of one's thinking and practice. He seemed to apprehend the difficulty of moving from a distinctly conceptual idea for a movement to one of practice. In birthing CFN and the idea of modern-day apostles, he would not avoid the intellectual rigor of rethinking the paradigm of church, recalibrating its governmental system, and reframing the essence of New Testament leadership. His desire was to move from a highly centralized form of organization to a more decentralized pattern. At the heart of his thinking, Sumrall embraced a decentralized ecclesiastical structure that would connect through a network of ministerial cells but would be formed around a centralized leader—the apostle.[52]

Sumrall inferred that the restoration of the fivefold ministry gifts embodied the movement of the Spirit of God for the church and would not be

51. Sumrall, *Apostolic Fathers and Their Families*, 62.
52. Brafman and Beckstrom, *Starfish and the Spider*, 164–75.

fully realized through the old organizational form of government. He was not against other forms of governmental structure or against structuring this new movement. He believed that the original New Testament church structure was very unlike the kind of structures that emerged in the church throughout its history. He simply believed that the apostolic paradigm was much better than the existing ones.

Sumrall was committed to birthing this new form of government that reintroduced the role of apostle back into the government of the church. The problem that he faced was that many viewed his outlook with an either/or perspective. Sumrall perceived the restoring of apostles and the apostolic movement in terms of both/and. As a restorationist, Sumrall believed that the answer for governmental ecclesiology was to embrace continuity *and* change, conservatism *and* progressiveness, stability *and* revolution, predictability *and* chaos, heritage *and* renewal.[53] This was not a hard issue for him. He recognized that God had invested his people with real potential, due largely to the ever-present kingdom of God, the lordship of Jesus Christ, the transforming power of the gospel, and the presence of the Holy Spirit in and among his people. Hence for Sumrall, restoring this apostolic environment was not something alien to the church; rather, what was needed was to reactivate what was already there in potential. For him, it meant simply triggering what was already present.

The apostle, together with the apostolic movement, was for Sumrall embedded in the New Testament origins. If rightly understood and implemented, it would inform innovative ethos and practices throughout the church world. It was the responsibility of the fivefold ministers/ministries to equip the saints and activate them into their calling. When purpose and principle were clearly understood and articulated, as well as commonly shared, the church would be healthy. To the degree that one held purpose and principle in common, one would dispense with command and control. Creativity is released. The church becomes a vital, living organism.

These ideas that Sumrall held can also be found in the business world. Dee Hock, CEO and founder of Visa credit card association, believed in the power of living beliefs. He stated,

> Purpose and principle, clearly understood and articulated, and commonly shared, are the genetic code of any healthy organization. To the degree you hold purpose and principles in common among you, you can dispense with command and control. People

53. Collins, "Building Companies to Last," para. 25.

will know how to behave in accordance with them, and they'll do it in thousands of unimaginable, creative ways. The organization will become a vital, living set of beliefs.[54]

Sumrall's major key to the network of cells within CFN was community—the power of godly relationships. Hock maintained the same idea in the business world. He stated, "All organizations are merely conceptual embodiments of a very old, very basic idea—the idea of community. They can be no more or less than the sum of the beliefs of the people drawn to them; of their character, judgments, acts, and efforts. An organization's success has enormously more to do with clarity of a shared purpose, common principles and strength of belief in them than to assets, expertise, operating ability, or management competence, important as they may be."[55] Hock called this the "chaordic principle," a portmanteau word formed by blending the terms "chaos" and "order." He maintained that every organization needed enough order at the center to give common identity and purpose, and enough chaos to give permission to creativity and innovation. This term fits well with Sumrall's understanding for a decentralized network of Christian ministerial cells. But before looking more closely at the network of CFN, space must be given for those who have voiced concerns over the fivefold ministry in the church and decentralized networks.

---

54. Hock, *Birth of the Chaordic Age*, 81–95.
55. Waldrop, "Dee Hock on Organization," para. 2.

7

Concerns and Apprehensions

THROUGHOUT CHRISTIAN HISTORY QUESTIONS have been asked that have led to new encounters for the believer and for the church. Essentially, this was happening at the beginning of the twentieth century with the birthing of the Pentecostal awakening. The idea of cessationism, which was embraced by the evangelical community, was challenged by Pentecostals. They bristled at the thought that the supernatural was limited just to the apostolic age. Advancing their restorationist views, they maintained a return to the apostolic faith of the New Testament. Moreover, they insisted that the description in the Book of Acts was intended to be the model through which the strength of the church should be measured today.

They were very much aware that without the power of the Spirit the church would lose its influence upon the world and become marginalized. This experience of restriction did not exempt any Christian tradition. Early Pentecostals, and later charismatics, strongly believed that the church must embrace a greater place for the supernatural capacity of the charismatic gifts and ministries.[1] Perhaps pragmatic considerations have forced much of the traditional church world into adopting charismatic practices, especially in the realm of worship. Notwithstanding, the Pentecostal and charismatic movements have occasioned new questions that required further reflection.

In its genesis, the Pentecostal revival employed the term "apostolic" both in their denominations and titles of periodicals. Associated with the term was the idea that the age of miracles was not past. The structure of church was not in need of adjustment as long as the existing governmental modalities made a place for the manifestations of the Spirit and

---

1. Ruthven, *On the Cessation of the Charismata*, 206.

the recognition of gifted ministries. Over time, the charismatic movement turned its attention to the inclusion of apostles in the fivefold ministry gifts of Eph 4:11–12. Starting with the Pentecostal revival of Azusa Street in 1906, the restoration of the charismata has led to the matter of the restoration of apostles to the church. Many have been attracted to the promise of newer church structures from the modern apostolic movement. However, concerns have been raised on how this "apostolic initiative" has been implemented. The following is a closer look at some of those apprehensions.

Vinson Synan

Synan has recently made several prophetic declarations concerning the future of the Pentecostal and charismatic renewal movement.[2] He concluded his remarks by stating that Pentecostals and charismatics have the opportunity to "reshape religion" in this century.[3] In contemplating this metamorphosis, Synan engaged the subject of modern-day apostles.

He admitted that nothing has stirred more recent interest in Pentecostal and charismatic circles as the restoration of the fivefold gifts that Paul mentioned in Eph 4:11–13. It stood to reason that the Ephesian church had a good understanding of Paul's meaning. However, with the passage of time, the role and activities of these ministries in the life of the church had become less clear.[4] Some believed that with the canon of Scripture the miraculous and the gifts of apostle and prophet had ceased.[5] Bishops had become primary in the church. However, throughout the history of the church, the idea of a continuing apostleship continued to arise.

Notwithstanding, Pentecostals and charismatics believed and taught that the gifts of the Spirit were present-day realities in the church. Because of this belief, many were asking, "If the *charismata* have been restored, why have not the prophets and apostles—those offices that the Lord himself set in the church—been restored also? As with the gifts of the Spirit, the dispensational limit on the exercise of these offices seemed to be man-made

---

2. Vinson Synan, "Charismatic Renewal after Fifty Years."

3. To underscore his point, Synan quotes from the subtitle of Harvey Cox's book *Fire from Heaven: The Rise of Pentecostal Spirituality and the Reshaping of Religion in the Twenty-First Century.*

4. Synan, "Who Are the Modern Apostles?" 42.

5. Synan, "Theological Boundaries," 47.

more than biblical."[6] As such, Synan asked, "What do apostles do to show they are *apostles*? If there are apostles today, *who* are they?"[7]

In answering these questions, Synan outlined what the Scriptures stated concerning apostles. He maintained the uniqueness of the original twelve apostles while underscoring the reality of "false apostles." For Synan, history revealed apostle-like ministries throughout the centuries. For example, St. Augustine of Canterbury was called the "apostle to England," and St. Patrick was called the "apostle to Ireland." Equally, Martin Luther could be seen as the "apostle of the Reformation," and Wesley could be known as the "apostle of Methodism."[8] In the end, Synan maintained that Pentecostals have been more interested in restoring the gifts of the Spirit than in restoring any type of ecclesiastical government to the church.[9]

A major concern for Synan was the views of C. Peter Wagner. Wagner maintained that the historical denominational churches were rapidly declining, and new post-denominational churches, which embraced the fivefold ministries of Eph 4:11–12, were dawning.[10] With his discipline in history, Synan pointed out that many whom Wagner claimed as part of the new apostolic movement were already part of the Pentecostal and charismatic renewal movement. Moreover, he questioned the need to charge fees to be a part of Wagner's International Coalition of Apostles. Subsequently, Synan listed nine reservations concerning the new apostolic movement.[11]

Synan argued that Wagner was trying to impose a new title for the movement that included dynamic churches originally inspired by the Pentecostals. For Synan, this movement failed to acknowledge the missionary accomplishment of the Pentecostals. Second, these networks were in fact incipient denominations. Even though they claimed to be only "apostolic networks" and developed structures under the claim of apostolic authority, they were in reality new denominations. Third, if apostles were given extra-local authority over congregations and their constituted leadership, it could cause confusion similar to the Shepherding Movement controversy

---

6. Synan, "Apostolic Practice," 14.

7. Ibid.

8. Ibid., 14–17.

9. Ibid., 19.

10. Wagner, *Churchquake!*, 38. Also see Wagner, *Changing Church*; Wagner, "Those Amazing Post-Denominational Churches"; Beckham, *Second Reformation*; and Hoefer, "New Times, New Structures."

11. Synan, "Apostolic Practice," 21–22.

of the 1980s. Fourth, there was a real danger for the apostles of these various networks to succumb to pride out of a lack of accountability. Fifth, all democratic or congregational government would end. The control of the church would be based in an apostolic hierarchy, with all authority vested in the top apostles. Sixth, territorial or extra-local apostles would be hard pressed to maintain viable relationships with their network leaders. Seventh, history reveals that apostolic movements of the past had very little growth. Eighth, leaders with too much authority and power have often yielded to pride. Last, proper protocol between denominations and apostolic networks has not been followed.[12]

Synan concluded by answering his original question, "Are there genuine apostles in the earth today?" He stated:

> The answer would seem to be yes—and no. No, there are no living persons like the original Twelve who witnessed the resurrection of Jesus Christ. These "apostles of Christ" were and will remain unique in salvation history. And, yes, there are apostles abroad today who are carrying out the same mission as the apostles in the New Testament. Who are they? The nearest parallel to the New Testament and historic use of the term "apostle" are those missionaries—often unnamed, untouted—who are bringing the message of the gospel for the first time to previously unreached peoples and tribes. They are busy translating the Scriptures and planting churches where none existed. They have little time to consider their apostolic office.[13]

Synan thereby equated the apostolic gift with an emphasis upon missionary effort. For him, the issue was not simply titles, but fruit. The real question for Synan was, "Where are the apostolic results?"

William Menzies

Early Pentecostals' fervent position on the supernatural dimension of Christianity caused most of the contemporary church world to take notice of charismatic gifts and ministries.[14] Philip Jenkins maintained that Christianity would continue to grow throughout the world and especially in the southern hemisphere. The Pentecostal and charismatic surge has brought

12. Ibid.
13. Ibid., 23.
14. Ruthven, *On the Cessation of the Charismata*, 206.

decades of change and promise that has swept this region. He stated, "The types of Christianity that have thrived most successfully in the global South have been very different from what many Europeans and North Americans consider mainstream. These models have been far more enthusiastic, much more centrally concerned with the immediate workings of the supernatural, through prophecy, visions, ecstatic utterances, and healings."[15]

Notwithstanding, it must be admitted that the presence or absence of the charismata in the believer's experience does not prove one's character or spiritual destiny. Nevertheless, the New Testament has shown a pattern as to how the gospel was to be presented, received, and lived out. All too often, believers tried "to reframe our failures into virtues, that is, by allowing what the NT describes as 'unbelief' in and for the gifts of God, to be constructed as having chosen 'the better way' of a 'stronger faith' without them."[16] If spiritual gifts were affirmed to be proof of one's spiritual condition, instead of tools for serving others, then conflict readily resulted. These thoughts echoed Menizes's concerns. Spiritual gifts were powerful weapons in advancing the kingdom of God. But if they were misused, they had the potential to wound and even destroy the people of God.

In the Pentecostal revival, the term "apostolic" was used to show that the Holy Spirit was being poured out and was empowering people in the same pattern that the authors of the New Testament described in the early life of the church. For Pentecostals, the word "apostolic" meant the proclamation that the age of the miracles was not past. In its early years, the Pentecostal contention was that one either accepted the paradigm of the availability of the New Testament experience of the Spirit or not. The restorationist debate centered on the re-examination of church governmental structures from which apostolic ministry was to be developed.[17] Pentecostals had described the office gifts of Ephesian 4 as "functions" rather than as "offices" of significant leaders. For example, Menzies observed that the Australian Assemblies of God had restructured its governmental leadership with a type of authority and responsibility that was associated with first-century apostles.[18] Hence, for Menzies, this required fresh reflection for the Pentecostal and charismatic church.

---

15. Jenkins, *Next Christendom*, 107.
16. Ruthven, *On the Cessation of the Charismata*, 107.
17. Menzies, "Apostolic in Doctrine," 27.
18. See Cartledge, *Apostolic Revolution*, 147–54.

Concerns and Apprehensions

Menzies approached his inquiry from a biblical perspective. Following Acts 2, Menzies summarized the primary characteristics of the early church. First, the Jerusalem church measured itself by teachings based upon the apostolic norm. Second, the Jerusalem church was keenly aware of God's supernatural presence. This *mysterium tremendum* was the hallmark of the early church and of Pentecostal fellowships in modern history. Third, signs and wonders marked the ministry of the early church. Apostles led the way, but it should be noted that other believers were involved in these as well. Stephen was a prime example, and Paul asserted that the full range of the charismata was available to all in the congregation—regardless of position or office (1 Cor 12:7–11). Fourth, believers gathered regularly expressing compassion and experiencing fellowship with the Lord and each other. Last, the major emphasis for the early church was community. As such, by the second century a separate level of ecclesiastical authority had been established.[19] Elders and overseers were terms used interchangeably.[20]

Moving to the Antioch church, Menzies used Acts 13:1–3 to compare two types of ministry structure—didactic and charismatic. He stated that in Antioch an attempt was made to maintain a balance between formal structure and spontaneous Charismatic ministry. The teachers of Acts 13 underscored the objective ministry of explaining the teachings of the apostles that had been passed on and mandated for study and preparation. The prophets stressed the subjective lifestyle of Christians and the immediacy of the charismatic gifts.[21] But for Menzies, this passage of Scripture provided a glimpse into the life of the church and a profile of the functions of that church body as well.[22]

The Antioch church highlighted the function of prophets and teachers as edifying the local church. Moreover, the purpose of the church was to minister to the Lord. Acts 13 emphasized the relationship between the believers and the risen Lord. Additionally, Menzies stated that the passage of Scripture revealed a ministry to the world. The apostolic church was a missionary church. In this Spirit-empowered ambience God gave direction

---

19. Menzies, "Apostolic in Doctrine," 28–29.

20. Arrington, *Maintaining the Foundations*, 74. Also see Arrington, *Christian Doctrine*, 3:175–85. French believes that the church is an apostolic community, and many leaders in the body of Christ act in an apostolic function (sent ones) but do not have the same authority as the original twelve (see pp. 181–82, 191–92).

21. Horton, *Book of Acts*, 155–56.

22. Menzies, "Apostolic in Doctrine," 30.

for service. The local church was at the heart of the sending, and this spoke of the principle of accountability for all leaders.[23]

Menzies traced this accountability through Paul's letters. For example, Paul sent Titus to appoint elders in the church that had been pioneered. Hence it seemed that at the earliest stages of a new church plant, it was necessary for extra-local leadership to help the church with directional issues. While Ephesus was not new, the people, with Timothy's approval, were mature enough to select leaders from among themselves (see 1 Tim 3:1). Menzies concluded that the local church moved from an episcopal form of outside leadership toward a congregational form as the church matured.[24] Likewise, he stated that Eph 4:12 describes leaders who were to empower God's people to do ministry. This revealed the objective of effective leadership, which was to build up the local church and local believers. The New Testament church was to include the capacity to grow, be self-perpetuating, and self-governing.[25]

From his biblical study, Menzies summarized four foundational principles for church structure. The first principle was apostolicity. All ministries were to be measured by those teaching which the Lord commissioned through the apostles. Second was the precept of adaptability. The Scriptures revealed considerable latitude in establishing church structure. Third was the principle of accountability. There were biblical evidences for a commitment to the responsibility of self-government within local churches. The people of God, for Menzies, had an important role in shaping this accountability, chiefly through their choice of elders and deacons who served in their midst.[26] Last was of the precept of accessibility. After the leadership of the apostles, there was minimal evidence of any hierarchy beyond the local church.[27]

From his biblical observations, Menzies had voiced his concerns over the "restorationism of modern-day apostles." He pointed out that recently the Australian Assemblies of God restructured itself by discarding the

---

23. Ibid.

24. Ibid., 32.

25. Hodges, *Indigenous Church and the Missionary*, 6–7.

26. Ladd, *Theology of the New Testament*, 388–91. Ladd maintained that once the church was successfully founded and the apostolic word of interpretation of the meaning of Christ was deposited in written form, no further need existed for the continuation of the apostolic office (390).

27. Menzies, "Apostolic in Doctrine," 34–35.

traditional pattern of ecclesiastical bureaucracy.[28] It has moved to displace its elected national and regional leadership with its centralized authority towards the autonomy of the local churches—a decentralized structure. They now recognized key pastors who exhibited "apostolic" authority. These leaders were usually the senior minister of large churches and small church pastors who came under their mentoring and nurture. While none of these leaders employ the term "apostle," they were readily acknowledged by others as exercising the office gift of apostle. Additionally, associated with this new leadership paradigm has been an emphasis upon the ministry of the prophet, through whom God speaks fresh revelation to the body of Christ.[29]

Another Australian leader, David Cartledge, taught a restorationism that advanced the efficacy of personal direction through prophetic words, the validity of modern-day apostles, and the need for "fresh revelation" through the ministries of modern-day prophets. Menzies had problems with Cartledge in several areas. First was Cartledge's high degree of subjectivity in what he called a Pentecostal hermeneutic.[30] Menzies also disagreed with the assertion that modern Pentecostals have the same relation with the Scriptures as the first-century apostles did.[31] Menzies was concerned that Cartledge failed to distinguish between the unique apostolic authority of the Bible from all other admissible revelation.[32] For Menzies, Cartledge opened the door for a disproportional level of subjectivism.

A further question that Menzies brought up was the possible abuse of power. With the setting aside of the standard Assemblies of God national church body, what would prevent abuses of governance by forceful leaders?[33] Menzies asked, "After all, who is going to dispute with an apostle?"[34]

28. Cartledge, *Apostolic Revolution*, 147–48.
29. Menzies, "Review of David Cartledge's *The Apostolic Revolution*," 334.
30. Cartledge, *Apostolic Revolution*, 174–75.
31. Ibid., 178.
32. Menzies, "Apostolic in Doctrine," 43. Also see McConnell, *Different Gospel*. McDonnell traces Hagin's beliefs to E. W. Kenyon, who introduced the concept of revelation knowledge as a fresh way of knowing the truth of Scripture. He pointed out that some in the faith movement advocated that esoteric experiences may furnish additional truth to supplement scriptural revelation, thereby implying that such contemporary revelations had equal validity with the Scriptures. McConnell referred to this as a "new Gnosticism" (103–13).
33. An insightful book on this subject is Cobble, *Church and the Powers*.
34. Menzies, "Apostolic in Doctrine," 43.

Finally, Menzies was troubled by C. Peter Wagner's position. First, he questioned Wagner's assumption that the authority of the original apostles extends to modern-day apostles. Menzies maintained that the original apostles had a unique authority that was only reserved for them. Wagner, on the other hand, stated, "Paul's authority as an apostle came from the same sources that provide today's apostles with their extraordinary authority."[35] Moreover, Menzies felt that Wagner confused the modern-day apostle with the gift of the missionary. He believed that there were specially gifted ambassadors who were sent out as missionaries.[36] Ultimately, Menzies believed that Wagner had blurred the boundaries between the unique twelve apostles and all other apostles—"sent ones" or frontier missionaries. As such, Menzies felt that Wagner had opened the door to abusive authority and power.

In the end, Menzies concluded that a case could be made for a difference between the original apostles of the New Testament and those who could be called apostles in a more general sense, especially when they are understood as emissaries of the local churches. But Menzies questioned the necessity to entitle these emissaries with the word "apostle." For him, the emphasis should be upon "apostolic function," rather than granting titles that might afford negative results. It is the function, not the name that was crucial for him.[37]

The Assemblies of God (USA)

While trying to balance their concerns for the spiritual revitalization for North American churches and avoiding the excesses of error and schisms of the New Order of the Latter Rain, the General Presbytery of the Assemblies of God (USA) advanced two major explanations concerning modern-day apostolic restorationism. The first was "Apostles and Prophets: A Position Paper," which was adopted by the General Presbytery on August 6, 2001.[38] The second was "Operational Definition: Apostolic Ministry and the U.S. Assemblies of God," which was approved by the Executive Presbytery on August 1, 2003.[39] Both of these papers clearly articulate the beliefs of the

---

35. Wagner, *Apostles and Prophets*, 26.
36. Menzies, "Apostolic in Doctrine," 41.
37. Ibid., 44–45.
38. Assembly of God General Council, *Apostles and Prophets: A Position Paper*.
39. Assembly of God General Council, *Minutes of the 50th Session*.

Concerns and Apprehensions

Assemblies of God concerning the restoration of modern-day apostles and prophets.

The Assemblies of God (AOG) have continued to carry the torch of the Pentecostal revival, which has been accompanied by a new openness to the gifts of the Spirit. In fact, it has been the AOG that has challenged the idea of cessationism in evangelical churches. With the restoration of the miraculous gifts to the church, the question had surfaced concerning the recovery of the fivefold ministry of Eph 4:11–12. Few dispute the validity of contemporary pastors, teachers, or evangelists. Many have called for the restoration of apostles and prophets.

The AOG stated that the adjective "apostolic" had several important insights. First was the idea of succession. Church bodies tried to connect their ministers back the original twelve. The Catholic and Episcopal churches do this. Second, Pentecostal churches have used the classification of "apostolic faith" to designate their unique doctrines. Third were the churches and networks that taught that God had raised up modern-day apostles. Last, most Protestant churches understand apostolic as the teaching of the original apostles, in other words, the New Testament doctrine.[40] Pentecostal believers understood themselves as apostolic because they had taught what the apostles taught, and they shared in the same power the apostles had through the baptism of the Holy Spirit. For them, the point was not contemporary apostles but apostolic doctrine and power.[41]

The AOG also maintained that the word "apostle" possibly carried the same meaning of the word *shaliach* in the Hebrew. *Shaliach* is a legal term that meant, "A man's agent is like unto himself."[42] It carried the same idea of the modern concept of power of attorney. For the AOG, the term carried with it the idea of a personal relationship with the Lord, preaching and teaching the kingdom of God, and demonstrating its power.

The AOG placed primary importance on the position of the original twelve. After the death of Judea, Scripture revealed the importance of the full complement of the original twelve. The twelve apostles of the New Testament was a symbol for the twelve tribes of Israel. After Pentecost, however, the Scripture displayed no effort to replace the original twelve or

---

40. Assembly of God General Council, *Apostles and Prophets*.
41. Ibid., 2.
42. Müller, "Apostle," 1:126–36.

to continue their number. For example, in Acts 12:2 no effort was made to replace James the brother of John when Herod killed him.[43]

In commenting on the other apostles mentioned in Scripture,[44] the AOG advanced the thoughts of E. Earle Ellis. He made a distinction between the "apostles of Christ" and the "apostles of the churches." The apostles of Christ were conferred to the disciple by the personal appearance and the commissioning of the Lord Jesus Christ and were unique to the first generation of believers. The identification of the apostles of the churches[45] was different and referred to anyone who was authorized and commissioned as missionaries.[46] The term was used to describe the "dispatching representatives on an official mission on behalf of the senders."[47]

In examining whether the apostolic gift of Eph 4:11–12 was passed on as a gift to the institutionalized church, the AOG gave a clear summary of the offices that were to function in the New Testament church. Citing the Book of Acts and the Pastoral Letters, they posited that elders were in leadership roles along with the apostles (Acts 11:30; 15:2; 16:4). Moreover, Paul was intentional in appointing elders for leaders in the churches he planted. In fact, Paul called for the elders at Ephesus and addressed them as overseers who were to shepherd them (Acts 20:28). Additionally, the Pastoral Epistles revealed Paul's concern for the appointment of elders, overseers, and deacons (1 Tim 3:1–12; Tit 1:3–9). It was clear from these scriptures that the appointment and continuation of these leaders were established for the local church then and now.[48]

The AOG advocated that from Scripture there was no provision for the replacement or continuation of the apostles. After Christ's resurrection, Scripture stated that he appeared to more than "five hundred of the brothers as the same time.... Then he appeared to James, then to all the apostles, and last of all he appeared to me also, as to one abnormally born" (1 Cor 15:6–8). From this scripture the AOG asserted that the gift of apostle was limited to those who had actually seen the Lord in the forty days after his

---

43. Assembly of God General Council, *Apostles and Prophets*, 3.

44. The New Testament makes mention of others who were, seemingly, understood to be apostles: James the brother of Jesus (1 Cor 15:7; Gal 1:19), Barnabas (Acts 14:14), Andronicus and Junias (who was probably a woman) were "outstanding among the apostles" (Rom 16:7).

45. See 2 Cor 8:23 and Phil 2:25.

46. Ellis, *Pauline Theology*, 38.

47. Assembly of God General Council, *Apostles and Prophets*, 4.

48. Ibid., 4–5.

resurrection. Nowhere in the New Testament, after the replacement of Judas, was there any emphasis upon apostolic succession. Notwithstanding, there were clear qualifications and instructions for the appointment of elders and deacons. It seemed "strange that apostles of Jesus Christ, concerned about faithful preservation of their message (cf. 2 Timothy 2:2), would provide for the appointment of overseers/elders while ignoring their own succession if such were indeed to be maintained."[49]

In dealing with the Eph 4:11–12 passage, the AOG stated those verses must be understood in the light of the entire book of Ephesians. While apostles were named first among the offices in the New Testament church, the context had already stated that the church was "built on the foundation of the apostles and prophets, with Christ Jesus himself as the chief cornerstone" (Eph 2:20). Moreover, Paul committed the leadership of the church to overseers/elders and deacons, not apostles and prophets.[50] There was a pointed progression of this leadership paradigm in Scripture. For example, the twelve called the Jerusalem church together to select the seven deacons (Acts 6). When they debated the Gentile matter in Acts 15, the issue was decided by the apostles and elders (vv. 4, 6, 22). When Paul returned from his third missionary journey, he called for "James and all the elders" (Acts 21:18). The absence of apostles on Paul's last journey confirmed that as the original twelve dispersed there was no need to provide for apostolic replacement. For the AOG, there was no reason for teaching the continual office gift of apostles.[51]

For the AOG, the apostles' authority allowed them to cross geographical lines, but they were aware of certain protocols in churches which they did not pioneer (Rom 15:20; 1 Cor 3:10). The New Testament revealed that their authority was universal concerning doctrinal and ethical issues. But there is little scriptural confirmation of their involvement in local administrative issues.[52] James D. G. Dunn echoed their conviction. He stated that Paul did not "think of apostolic authority as something exercised by individuals throughout all the churches. As apostolic authority was subordinate to the gospel, so it was limited by the scope of apostolic commission."[53]

---

49. Ibid., 5. Also see Fee, *First Epistle to the Corinthians*, 732.
50. Müller, "Apostle," 1:135.
51. Assembly of God General Council, *Apostles and Prophets*, 5–6.
52. Ibid., 6.
53. Dunn, *Theology of Paul the Apostle*, 579. Moreover, Dunn stated, "apostolic authority is exercised not over the Christian community, but within it; and the authority is

From their scriptural enquiry, the AOG made several statements concerning the chief characteristics that would identify a genuine apostle. First was that an apostle had seen the Lord and been personally commissioned by him as a witness to his resurrection. Second was that the apostle had received the baptism of the Holy Spirit and was granted the gift of apostleship. Third, apostles were supernaturally equipped for prophetic preaching and teaching. Fourth, apostles were endowed with miraculous power for signs, wonders, and miracles. Fifth, apostles were responsible for the accuracy and purity of the gospel. Sixth, apostles were commissioned to plant churches and operated as missionaries. Seventh, apostles suffered for the gospel. Last, apostles were very pastoral and relational.[54]

Turning their attention to the gift of the prophet, the AOG recognized the role of the New Testament prophet in the early church. From their biblical analysis, the AOG made the following conclusions concerning prophets. First, Scripture attests to prophets in the early church, who often worked closely with apostles. Second, apostles oftentimes functioned as prophets (Acts 13:1; 15:32; Rev 1:3). Third, prophets traveled from church to church. Fourth, the biblical account revealed that both men and women were seen as prophets. Fifth, prophets exercised spiritual influence with apostles and elders in the practice and belief of the early church. Sixth, the prophet's integrity was measured against the scriptures and the apostolic doctrine. Last, the AOG saw no stipulation for appointing prophets as part of a church's leadership hierarchy for succeeding generations.[55]

While the AOG did not embrace the office gift of the prophet for the modern-day church, they did see the gift of prophecy as part of the gifts of the Spirit. Every believer received the power of the Spirit to be a prophetic witness to the resurrection of Jesus Christ. They embraced the belief that all believers were invested into a universal prophethood,[56] and all believers should "earnestly desire the gift of prophecy" (1 Cor 14:1).[57]

---

exercised (in the words of Ephesians) 'to equip the saints for the work of ministry, for the building up of Christ's body' (Eph. 4:12)" (574).

54. Assembly of God General Council, *Apostles and Prophets*, 7–8.

55. Ibid., 9.

56. Stronstad, *Prophethood of All Believers*, 71–84. Stronstad states, "No longer is the prophetic ministry limited to an individual, or to a select group, but it is now the reality for all God's people—a veritable nation of prophets" (84).

57. For examples of the prophetic phenomena in the modern church, see Lindblom, *Prophecy in Ancient Israel*, 13–18; Blessitt, *Turned on to Jesus*, 90–95, 130; Ellis, "Prophecy in the New Testament Church."

Concerns and Apprehensions

In concluding their observations regarding modern-day apostles and prophets, the AOG made several remarks that have had a doctrinal impact upon the denomination. Additionally, they sought to answer several questions about apostles and prophets for their local congregations.

From their inspection of Scripture, they made the following statements. First, Scripture did not furnish enough instruction for the appointment of future apostles and prophets for contemporary offices in governing the church. Second, while it is certainly not necessary, some churches may choose to name certain leaders "apostles." The AOG accepted the distinction between "apostles of Jesus Christ" and "apostles of the churches," but such leaders will not have seen the risen Lord in the same manner as the original apostle. Moreover, their teachings will not add to the canon of Scripture. Third, leaders who have been granted the title of "apostle" should remember that historically apostles have been people of stalwart character and great effectiveness in the church. The AOG readily recognized that some individuals who have been so entitled can be tempted to assert dominance and control over the believers, while not being accountable to the members in their care or to their local leadership. Fourth, the Scripture revealed that the function of apostles was to plant churches and to minister to the unevangelized. Last, the AOG stated that the gift of prophecy was an ongoing gift of the Holy Spirit. The Spirit will continue to choose men and women to give this gift for the purpose of "strengthening, encouraging, and comforting" the body of Christ (1 Cor 14:3). Howbeit, the content of the prophecy should always be tested by and responsible to the authority of the Scripture.[58] They concluded their position with this penetrating statement: "Some apostolic and prophetic functions flowing from persons directly commissioned by the risen Lord and acting in revelatory capacities seem clearly to belong to the foundational era of the Church. At the same time, some of those functions having to do with the revitalization, expansion, and nurture of the church ought to be present in every generation."[59]

Endeavoring to bring clarity, the AOG answered three questions for their churches and for the public at large. They were: (1) Does the Assemblies of God recognize present-day apostles and prophets? (2) What is the implication for the local church in the current emphasis on apostles and

---

58. Assembly of God General Council, *Apostles and Prophets*, 9–10.
59. Ibid., 10–11.

prophets? (3) Should Assemblies of God churches welcome the ministries of apostles and prophets?[60]

In answering the first question, the AOG stated they believed the local church was governed by overseers/elders and deacons. They stated that this practice was consistent with the apostolic witness given in 1 and 2 Timothy and Titus. Moreover, the apostles did not appoint apostles and prophets for the local church but elders. Hence, within the AOG leaders will not be recognized by the title of apostle or prophet. But the AOG admitted to an apostolic function, which is related to planting new works and ministering among unreached people. Concerning prophecy, the AOG embraced the gift of prophecy found in 1 Corinthians 12. Its function is to strengthen, encourage, or comfort. But they hold that any predictive prophecy that departed from Scripture and proved false led to the conclusion that the person was a "false prophet" (Deut 18:19–22). In the end, the AOG focused upon the function of one's ministry. The title does not make the person.[61]

The AOG answer to their second question was congregational government. Their understanding of the fivefold ministry was found in Eph 4:12—to prepare God's people for works of service. The stress was upon every believer's ministry. In fact, the growth of the Pentecostal revival came from the Spirit-filled ministry of all believers. The AOG has overwhelmingly embraced the "priesthood of all believers." They concluded that they "look with grave concern on those who do not believe in congregational church government, who do not trust the maturity of local church bodies to govern themselves under Scripture and the Spirit."[62]

In answering their third question, the AOG stated that any leader from outside the AOG should be thoroughly investigated as to their teaching and character before being allowed to minister in any AOG church. Such a person may bring confusion and problems into the local church. It was their recommendation that AOG churches use AOG ministers.[63]

Finally, the AOG's Executive Presbytery approved an "Operational Definition" for the exercise an apostolic ministry within their ministry on August 1, 2003, during their fiftieth session of the General Council, in Washington, DC. From 2001 to 2003, the AOG seemed to embrace the function of the apostolic ministries within its denomination. The definition

60. Ibid., 11–12.
61. Ibid., 11.
62. Ibid.
63. Ibid., 12.

stated: "biblical apostolic ministry is marked by God-sent, church recognized leaders whose ministry, through the anointed proclamation of the gospel, with accompanying signs and wonders, results in the expansion of the kingdom of God."[64]

This definition was based upon their understanding of the apostolic function as revealed by the early church. First, the apostolic function depended completely upon the Holy Spirit and his power for the release of this gift. Second, the description included that this function centered upon reaching the unevangelized. Thereby, their stress was upon missionary endeavors. Third, they understood the apostolic function to include relationship building, especially through mentoring. Fourth, the function purpose was to equip, empower, and release new generations of leaders. Hence, those who operated with an apostolic function tended to be leaders of leaders. Fifth, they focused upon planting churches that would become self-supporting and reproducing New Testament congregations. Sixth, were to produce lasting fruit through the duplication of more churches being birthed. Last, leaders who operated with the apostolic function did not aspire to either the office or title of "apostle." They embodied responsibility, accountability, and humility with the local church.[65]

While the AOG USA does not hold to the office gift of apostle for the contemporary church, this "Operational Statement" indicates that they have accepted that there are those who operate with an apostolic function. Perhaps with the huge growth of the AOG Australia, which has embraced the apostolic function for today and as a result has birthed many churches there and abroad, the AOG USA has encouraged apostolic function within their congregations.

Synopsis and Review

In this chapter we reviewed how Synan surveyed apostolic ministries throughout church history. He traced the restorationist movement of the nineteenth century and into the Pentecostal revival of the twentieth century. He provided insightful comparison of the new apostolic movement with the growth of the Pentecostal revival. His areas of concerned underscored the necessity of fruit over titles.

64. Assembly of God General Council, *Minutes of the 50th Session*, "Operational Definition," 69.
65. Ibid.

William Menzies appraised the Book of Acts by comparing the Jerusalem church with the Antioch church. He focused upon how apostolic authority functioned in those churches. He surveyed the ministries of the apostles of the early church, showing their scope and level of authority. This background served as a foil for examining the apostolic restorationist movement.

The changes in the AOG Australia have presented ecclesiastical challenges for the AOG USA concerning church structure over the Eph 4:11–12 paradigm. They have raised old and new questions for church governing policies and church growth.

The insights of this chapter reflect the struggles that CFN has wrestled with and the ecclesiastical changes they have embraced. It has been the leadership of L. A. Joiner and Buford Lipscomb that has helped CFN answer those encapsulating questions that have ensued from the apostolic restorationist movement: Are there apostles in the church today? What relationship do these apostles have with the institutional church? How do we recognize genuine apostolic ministries? The next chapter examines both Joiner's and Lipscomb's leadership of CFN, their fundamental convictions, and the changes which they embraced.

8

Leadership and Directional Changes for Church Foundational Network

KEN SUMRALL UNDERSTOOD THAT there would be those who either did not understand the direction of CFN or would not embrace the fivefold ministry of Eph 4:11–12. The restorationist movement, for Sumrall, was a move from a centralized form of church government to a decentralized form. He assumed there would be opposition to these changes. After operating for twenty years under a centralized ecclesiastical governmental structure with a measure of success, he was all too familiar with the human condition of resistance to change. It would be difficult at best for a maintenance-oriented leadership organization to embrace the changes needed for a decentralized, apostolic network to work properly. The majority of Liberty Fellowship did not agree with Sumrall, and they did not discern any reason for replacing their existing leadership paradigm. But Sumrall was convinced that he had perceived the plan of God and was not called to maintain the status quo for the sake of unity, and CFN was birthed in 1995.[1]

Sumrall was confident that governmental change was coming to the church. The bureaucracy within the governing of the church needed to be adjusted. Alvin Toffler in *Future Shock* argued for a more relational form of organizational structure decades before Sumrall developed his position. He stated, "The acceleration of change has reached so rapid a pace that even bureaucracy can no longer keep up." He contended that "newer . . . more instantly responsive forms of organization must characterize the future." He believed that society was witnessing the "collapse of hierarchy" because "shortcuts that by-pass the hierarchy are increasingly employed" in many types of organizations. "The cumulative result of such small changes is a

---

1. Sumrall, *Apostolic Fathers and Their Families*, 4–5.

massive shift from vertical to lateral communication systems."[2] Toffler pointed out that organizational bureaucracy was passing away as many cultural norms were moving into a post-industrial season. Hence, this would be highly significant for denominational and other ecclesiastical organizations and could move the church into a post-denominational phrase.[3] Moreover, institutions and structures were not themselves the church. For Sumrall, CFN was the embodiment of this post-denominational paradigm. He held to a firm belief that, whatever happened to or in the church, the new network of churches was to be charismatic. For Sumrall, men were created to have fellowship with God, and this fellowship was to be filled with the supernatural power of God. Sumrall saw two paths: go forth with charismatic, apostolic networks or lose its charismatic dimension by succumbing to an ecclesiastical hierarchy of political ladder climbing.[4] His forecast for the future of CFN rested upon his successors: L.A. Joiner and Buford Lipscomb.

L. A. Joiner

After a short stint in the navy, Joiner began training for the ministry under senior pastor Edward Robbins of Waycross, Georgia, at El Bethel Christian Assembly. He was twenty-three years old. For four years (1972–1976) Joiner worked at a secular job while working at the church, primarily volunteering for various positions and opportunities. He finally became the "student pastor," which meant that he was seen as an official trainee for the ministry. It was at this time that the charismatic revival was in full swing. During this revival, Joiner met William (Bill) Ligon, who had recently received the baptism of the Holy Spirit and started a new charismatic church in Brunswick, Georgia, called Christian Renewal Center. They began meeting together for fellowship and prayer. Out of these meetings, the Fellowship of Charismatic Churches and Ministers International was birthed. Later the group was renamed as the Fellowship of Churches and Ministers.[5]

In 1977, at the age of twenty-seven, he was released to plant his first church, El Bethel Church in Hazelhurst, Georgia,.[6] After getting El

2. Toffler, *Future Shock*, 139, 143.
3. Ibid., 126–27.
4. Sumrall, *Apostolic Fathers and Their Families*, 73.
5. Joiner, email message to author, August 27, 2013.
6. Joiner, "Back-Seater."

Leadership and Directional Changes

Bethel established, Joiner moved to Brunswick, Georgia, in 1979. Ligon had been researching the Shepherding Movement for several years, and finally published his book *Discipleship: The Jesus View (An Alternative to Extremism)*.[7] In the book, Ligon took issue with the teachings of the Shepherding Movement, and Joiner was aware of Ligon's position and views. Interesting enough, Ken Sumrall wrote an endorsement for the book. Joiner and Sumrall were getting to know each other during his time in Waycross.

In 1980, when Joiner birthed New Covenant Christian Center in Valdosta, Georgia, he was very careful to maintain a "missional mindset" and steered clear of the Shepherding Movement controversy. During his early years in Valdosta, Joiner's emphasis was on winning souls and church planting. Several years later the church was named New Covenant Church. New Covenant became the "mother church" for Joiner's ministerial cell, named Christian Alliance of Ministers, which he founded in 1999 and became affiliated with CFN.[8]

However, Joiner's mindset began to change towards the Shepherding Movement, especially concerning the concept of discipleship through relationships. This milestone started for Joiner when he met Dr. H. Young Tillman. Tillman, a local dentist, was born again during the charismatic renewal of the late 1960s. He eventually connected with the Shepherding Movement and became an elder with Christian Home Ministries of Valdosta, Georgia. From the Shepherding Movement's discipleship paradigm, Tillman learned the importance of relational government. However, Tillman pointed out that if one was not careful, discipleship could produce an inward attitude at the expense of reaching out into one's community. By the early 1980s the leadership of Christian Home Ministries understood that its members had become too inward in their thinking concerning the kingdom of God. The decision was made to join New Covenant Church (NCC), which Joiner was pastoring at the time, because NCC had a more outward focus of bringing the church into the world. On the other hand, NCC was weak in its discipleship training. Tillman recalled the merger a "mutual benefit."[9]

---

7. Ligon, *Discipleship*. See Barrs, *Shepherds and Sheep*, for concerns of hierarchical leadership structures, coverings, and the chain-of-command principles that he taught were distorted.

8 For more detail of Joiner's journey from Liberty Fellowship of Ministers and Church into Church Foundational Network, see chapter 5.

9. Tillman, interview with author, February 11, 2013.

In 1983 Christian Home Ministries joined en masse with New Covenant. Overnight, NCC doubled in size. Through the next couple of years, several of the Christian Home Ministries leaders were asked to be elders of NCC. Tillman was one of them. He immediate understood that the leadership was very good at giving guidance to the church. But the relational issues within the leadership were weak. Their elder's meetings were more like business meetings, with very little deep friendships being made.[10] The rest of the leadership of NCC agreed. They began adjusting their leadership structure and intentionally started spending more personal time together. The point was to move beyond a business mentality of church government towards a relational form of government. Trust needed to be built between them as leaders.[11]

Joiner recalled the merger as very healthy for the church. But he admitted that the first year of that alliance was difficult as members were getting to know one another. Tillman was the catalyst in changing some of Joiner's paradigms on church government and his thinking towards Shepherding Movement principles. Joiner remembered Tillman's concerns for the eldership. "Young was the one who kept pressing us to go away and spend time together on a regular basis in order to build stronger relationships."[12] It was through Tillman that Joiner admitted that he learned that New Testament government was relational and not political. Moreover, Joiner believed that their emphasis on relational government proved invaluable through the years by helping them weather several storms. In fact, NCC never had a split or major group leave that wasn't planned as multiplication.

Joiner admitted that he struggled with learning how to trust and how to build a team mentality in their leadership structure. Furthermore, he attributed their governmental success to Tillman and Bill Thomas, another local dentist and Christian Home Ministries leader. Joiner stated, "Young and later Bill Thomas helped me get a handle on it, primarily because they proved their love for me; and they only wanted the common good."[13] Joiner summed up what he learned from the brothers of the Shepherding Movement, particularly the fruit of the Spirit that developed as they walked together:

10. Ibid.
11. Ibid.
12. Joiner, email message to author, January 23, 2013.
13. Ibid.

Leadership and Directional Changes

1. Deeper levels of worship
2. Corporate release of the gifts and a move toward spontaneity in services
3. Biblical government
4. Better development of the individual member (discipleship)
5. How to confront without conflict (biblically)
6. Covenant relationships[14]

He admitted that there were a few negatives that resulted from the merger. Some cliques tried to form, but the leadership was able to emphasize the church's vision over them. They desired a completely homogenous group and not a church within a church.[15]

Around 1985, Sumrall introduced Joiner to Charles Simpson of Mobile, Alabama, and they became friends. After their reconciliation, Simpson looked to Sumrall as his pastor.[16] Over time, Joiner came to embrace the teachings of the Shepherding Movement and discerned its compatibility with relational, apostolic government. He particularly identified with its teaching that the local church was the vehicle of God's kingdom expressed on earth, and its stress on the nature of the local church as the essential character of the kingdom of God.[17] He would often defend Simpson's teaching on discipleship. For Joiner, the issue was not what Simpson taught, but the many immature leaders within the Shepherding Movement. He believed that "an underdeveloped leadership gift or one that has never been discipled under the oversight and discipline of a loving spiritual father is a dangerous and often destructive thing."[18] Joiner held to these convictions throughout his involvement in CFN. He taught that for godly, apostolic government to work it would require submission. For Joiner, submission was not true submission unless it was tested. Everyone needed to be accountable.[19] Notwithstanding, the Shepherding Movement taught that submission involved a thoughtful recognition of the one God had placed over

---

14. Ibid.
15. Ibid.
16. Joiner, email message to author, September 23, 2013.
17. Muford, "Vision of the Local Church," 4–8.
18. Joiner, "Turning Leaders into Leaders."
19. Joiner, "When Others Interfere."

the believer and required a deeper level of transparency and openness for pastoral care.[20]

Joiner became the president of CFN in 2005. He made no significant changes to CFN during his tenure as president. Part of this reason was that Sumrall was still on the CFN council at the time, even though his health was beginning to deteriorate. For his part, Sumrall had a difficult time releasing the leadership to Joiner. But Joiner was satisfied to continue his focus upon the local church during his tenure with CFN.[21] Joiner had such respect and honor for Sumrall that he never challenged him or pulled rank on him. In concluding his time as president of CFN, Joiner summarized his tenure:

> As I ended my role as Executive Director I realized that my role had been one of holding the football until Papa Ken was truly ready for someone else to take it in a new direction. That probably wouldn't happen as long as he was living. I could tell that he was trying to release it but it wasn't a complete work in his heart. I was at peace with maintaining his vision and philosophy of ministry. For example, he was committed to CFN being "decentralized" and not a group with a centralized vision or emphasis. He didn't believe that we should plant churches as a group but should support the apostolic cells and network the cells without directing them and honoring their autonomy. There would be meetings where he would say, "L. A. is going to lead the meeting." Then he would take over the meeting. I don't say that with any malice at all. I would just sit back and smile as others around the table would look at me and smile. We all knew it wasn't over yet because he still had an inner drive to lead but no natural energy. I knew that I had grace to do it and I did it for five years. I didn't want anyone else to take it and dishonor him in his last days. I'm not trying to be a martyr here but that was my heart and it was easy to do. I had no desire or ambition to lead CFN outside that role. It was necessary for that transitional hour. I didn't at all feel like I was living under his shadow. It was an honor to carry his coat! At the end he asked me to become the President but I knew that wasn't my grace to do so. I can't build on another man's foundation and that has always been my posture. I'm more of a foundation layer that a reconstruction man.[22]

Not many leaders would have had the patience that Joiner had with Sumrall. The love between the two of them was evident to all who knew them.

20. Mumford, *LifeChangers*, 5.
21. Lipscomb, interview with author, February 18, 2013.
22. Joiner, email message to author, April 24, 2013.

Leadership and Directional Changes

In planning for this transfer of leadership, Joiner had summarized his thoughts earlier. He conceived his understanding in terms of a relay race:

> Here's the really hard part: in a relay race the one running passes the baton to the next runner and the first runner stops running. In the generational transfer, the older runner doesn't stop, he passes the baton and allows (empowers) the younger runner to run faster than he and yet there remains this heart connection of continuing to pass on the wisdom of the past to the zeal of the future. It takes supernatural humility to do either. The older will see the new runner taking his race to a new level. He will see him do it with a new style that the older runner never saw and hopefully, at a new record. The younger runner must make the decision to look back to the old for wisdom and direction that only experience can bring. He must seek it out![23]

In the end, Sumrall was unable to release completely the reins of CFN to Joiner. Notwithstanding, Joiner did continue to underscore the importance of the local church and the concept of the apostolic paradigm.

Another milestone in Joiner's philosophy of ministry occurred in the early 1990s. At the encouragement of Dr. Young Tillman, Joiner invited Dr. Costa S. Deir to come and speak at a conference at NCC. In addressing the greatest need for the church, Deir stated, "the greatest need in the world is not evangelism. The greatest need in the world is leadership development!" He went on to say, "If you reach one soul for the Lord, that is a wonderful thing but if your reach and train a leader, you have reached potentially thousands." Joiner stated that those few statements changed him and his focus for ministry.[24] From this point forward, Eph 4:11–12 and the fivefold ministry became central for Joiner's understanding of the church. The church was to be a training center for equipping the saints and releasing leaders. The fivefold ministries were the leadership team needed in the local church for effective expansion of the kingdom of God. Joiner soon started a "school of ministry" at NCC to facilitate training leaders. Evangelism, for Joiner, was the result of successfully training of leaders for ministry. Consequently, Joiner's outward aim from his earlier years at NCC continued as he added an inward concentration—the primacy of the local church as an equipping center.

---

23. Joiner, "'Kingdom Stuffs' Part 2."
24. Joiner, "Greatest Need."

Despite the appropriateness of the kingdom of God concept, Joiner's integrative motif for how it operated in the world was through the local church—the community of God. For Joiner, one's personal growth and development was grounded in the local church from which he lived out his convictions.[25] The local church was responsible for transmitting to its members the virtue, common good, and ultimate meaning of the gospel. For Joiner, this not only formed his convictions; it was a central message of the Bible. Taken as a whole, the Bible declared that God's design was to bring into being community in its highest sense—a reconciled people, living within a renewed creation, and enjoying the presence of their redeemer.[26] The church was a community in Joiner's understanding. Attending meetings alone did not constitute community. Quality time must be spent together to form true community. Joiner believed that real community in the local church was a sharing of life that impacted and changed the believer for their own improvement and good.[27] George Lindbeck held that the community of the local church offered to the believer a tradition of virtue and meaning.[28] Joiner would agree and insisted that believers become incorporated into the life of the local church and be discipled through committed relationships—a conviction Joiner shared with the Shepherding Movement.[29]

The key to Joiner's leadership matrix was committed relationships, especially for the apostolic counsel and for each ministerial cell of CFN. He believed that we had become a throwaway society where even friendships were temporary. Commitments to friends, job, community, and family were on the decline, and within the United States the ideal man stood alone, self-sufficient and autonomous.[30] During his tenure at CFN Joiner taught that church government should be relational, first and foremost. Loving and trusting God and others was fundamental for this relational paradigm. C. S. Lewis stated in *The Four Loves* that loving is risking. He stated,

> To love at all is to be vulnerable. Love anything, and your heart will certainly be wrung and possibly be broken. If you want to make sure of keeping it intact, you must give your heart to no one, not even to an animal. Wrap it carefully round with hobbies and little

---

25. MacIntyre, *After Virtue*, 221.
26. Genz, *Theology for the Community of God*, 23–24.
27. Joiner, "Community."
28. Lindbeck, "Confession and Community," 495.
29. Prince, *Discipleship, Shepherding, Commitment*, 46.
30. Toffler, *Future Shock*, 51–73.

Leadership and Directional Changes

luxuries; avoid all entanglements; lock it up safe in the casket—safe, dark, motionless, airless—it will change. It will not be broken; it will become unbreakable, impenetrable, irredeemable.[31]

Not embracing committed relationships was what Joiner understood would lead to a political environment in governing a church. Joiner's governmental paradigm for the local church was grounded in his views on the doctrine of salvation. Salvation was a relationship. The church was built on the revelation that Jesus is the Son of God, and believers needed to move beyond only keeping the rules and regulations and enter that place of intimacy with Jesus.[32] For apostolic government to function, Joiner knew that great trust needed to be developed between the leadership team of the apostolic council. He posited several characteristics for building an apostolic council for each ministerial cell. The following were some of his insights: correctly choosing the right leaders; spending as much time as needed in order to develop respect and trust (time was the cost of every relationship); develop and honor confidentiality; committing to preferring others above yourself; believing that other members of the team were in the will of God by being on the team; and continuing to trust, especially in confrontations.[33] Frank Damazio stated that no member was more important than another, but that for the sake of order and efficiency someone must be chosen as the key leader with final responsibility. Failure to recognize the senior leader within the team could lead to severe problems.[34] For Joiner, this key leader was the apostle.

Another ecclesiological shift for Joiner was the necessity for a decentralized church government structure. In July 2003 Sumrall appointed Joiner, with the approval of the apostolic council of CFN, to be his successor when the time came for him to step down as the apostolic father of CFN. Together, they were determined that CFN would not become centralized in its governmental structure, much like a denomination. Instead CFN embraced a decentralized government structure that functioned with the paradigm of Eph 4:11–12. CFN and all its ministerial cells were led by modern-day apostles within the framework of each cell being seen as a family and its lead apostle as the father. Practically speaking, this meant

---

31. Lewis, *Four Loves*, 169.
32. Joiner, "Intimacy or Intimidation."
33. Joiner, "Trust . . . Foundation of Team."
34. Damazio, *Making of a Leader*, 280.

the apostle being there, leading, motivating, imparting vision, and giving encouragement. Sometimes it required correction, but never control.[35]

The covenant that each apostolic cell of CFN committed to was the following:

1. We commit ourselves to be servants and not controllers (Phil 2:5).
2. We commit ourselves to always pioneer new frontiers, never settling down.
3. We commit ourselves to continue mentoring, discipling, training, and equipping people to minister so they will *not* simply be sponges that absorb truth and never deliver it to others. Rather, they will be trained to be doers of the Word.
4. We commit ourselves to major on imparting, not just on informing. Our aim is to impart gifts, grace, faith, boldness, and vision.
5. We commit ourselves to mature and establish people so they do not remain babies on milk but become an army to overcome the enemy.
6. We commit ourselves to be a people ready to take risks, and not just to play it safe within our comfort zones.
7. We commit ourselves to keep passion of the Lord for a lost world.
8. We commit ourselves to be a people of prayer.
9. We agree that the church should be set in order with apostolic government so the world can see the order of God in operation.[36]

It should be noted, however, that CFN and its apostolic cells did not plant churches. Church planting was left up to the individual local churches. To become a church planting network was, for Joiner, too centralized.

Joiner resigned from leading CFN in 2009 due to health issues and his desire to focus more on his own apostolic cell. He stated:

> Two things have caused me to have to reevaluate priorities in my life and ministry. My ongoing health challenges have brought me to a place of limited physical resources. The second thing is the continued increasing demand that my cell, Christian Alliance of Ministries, requires of me. I have more and more leaders who desire more involvement from me in their ministries. I want very

---

35. Sumrall, *Apostolic Fathers and Their Families*, 73, 81.
36. Ibid., 77–78.

much to have time and energy to give to them and to see them rise to their full potential.[37]

He resigned from the CFN apostolic council in 2009, and he has been leading his ministerial cell since then. When Joiner stepped down as the president of CFN, he and Simpson conferred with Sumrall concerning Buford Lipscomb replacing Joiner and becoming the next president of CFN. Sumrall agreed.

Buford Lipscomb

Lipscomb was raised in the Atlanta suburb of Cartersville, Georgia. He married his childhood sweetheart, Ann, in 1970. He soon felt the call into Christian ministry, and Ann and he became the interim pastor of Victory Temple in Cartersville. They moved to Pensacola, Florida, to attend Liberty Bible College in 1979.[38] Sumrall told Lipscomb about a church startup in Fairhope, Alabama, and strongly encouraged him to go there. Lipscomb agreed and spent ten years there.[39]

After Sumrall resigned from Liberty Church, it split.[40] In 1992 Lipscomb moved back to Pensacola to become the interim pastor of Liberty. Lipscomb recalled that first Sunday as a great challenge. "The church sat 2000, but only one hundred and fifty showed up the first Sunday after the split."[41] Remaining faithful, the church started growing after Lipscomb had been there for five years. With this momentum, Lipscomb convinced the leadership to sell Liberty Bible College to the Brownsville Revival School of

37. Joiner, letter to Ken Sumrall, November 15, 2009, private holding.

38. Collins and Caroline, "Senior Moments," 1. Lipscomb has a bachelor's degree from Liberty Bible College and a PhD in Christian education from Liberty Christian College (1998). Additionally, he has served on the board of directors of Waldorf College in Forest City, Iowa, since 2009.

39. Lipscomb, interview with author, February 18, 2013. By the end of his tenure in Fairhope, Alabama, Lipscomb was the distinct overseer with Liberty Fellowship of Ministers and Churches (LFMC).

40. Sumrall was beginning to have some health issues and want to spend more time with those with whom he had graduated from Liberty Bible College and were in the ministry. He made John Havner, who was the singles pastor, the senior pastor. This proved to be a hasty decision, and the church began to decline. Sumrall came back to the church, but this was not well received. Havner left and started another church, and many people went with him. Dr. Larry Hart was asked to lead the church after Havner, but the church continued to decline. Dr. Hart left Liberty Church and is now teaching at ORU.

41. Lipscomb, interview with author, February 18, 2013.

Ministry. With the funds from the sale of the property, they moved to the Blue Angel Parkway and built the present Liberty campus in 2001.[42]

In 1995 Sumrall began CFN. Lipscomb pointed out that Sumrall was sixty-nine years old when he started CFN. He did not want the focus to be upon him but upon his "spiritual sons." These sons would relate to Sumrall as their apostle (spiritual father) and they, in turn, would have their own ministerial cells. By contrast, LFMC was all about Sumrall being the leader. Sumrall desired a more organic structure for church government—a decentralized structure. Lipscomb maintained that Simpson was very influential in helping Sumrall develop his governmental understanding. Indeed, CFN was to be a healthier form of the original Shepherding Movement, especially in the area of relational oversight. CFN was to learn from some of the failures of the Shepherding Movement and better embody the concepts of discipleship and accountability. In fact, Sumrall invited Simpson to sit in on the CFN leadership council meetings. In 2010 Lipscomb replaced Joiner as the president of CFN, and in 2012 he invited Simpson to join the CFN leadership. Simpson accepted.[43]

In 2005 Lipscomb felt lead to start a Liberty campus church each year for the next five years. By 2010, he had reached his goal. These churches included North Liberty campus; Liberty campus Fairhope, Alabama; Liberty campus Navarre, Florida; Liberty campus Foley, Alabama; and Liberty campus Mobile, Alabama.[44] From these churches Lipscomb formed his own network of churches named Liberty Network, which presently has over ninety-three pastors and ministers. Liberty Network is one of the ministerial cells of CFN. Moreover, under his leadership CFN has grown to six hundred ministers.[45]

On January 11, 2013, Ken Sumrall passed away at the Healthcare Center of Pensacola, Florida. He was in hospice care at the time.[46] Up till his death, Lipscomb was very careful to honor Sumrall and his direction for CFN. Howbeit, Lipscomb had begun to cast vision concerning CFN expanding, especially by focusing on church planting and by bolstering the number

---

42. Lipscomb, interview with author, February 12, 2013.

43. Lipscomb, interview with author, February 18, 2013; and Simpson, interview with author, March 9, 2012.

44. Collins and Caroline, "Senior Moments," 1.

45. Lipscomb, interview with author, February 21, 2012.

46. Williams, email message to author, January 11, 2013. Williams is Joiner's personal secretary. Sumrall was eighty-six years old at the time of his death.

Leadership and Directional Changes

of ministerial cells. The June 2013 CFN conference was the occasion that Lipscomb advanced some significance changes for the overall network.

Upon stepping down from CFN, Sumrall had stated that he was satisfied that God had his own plans regarding the continuation of CFN. He even suggested the possibility of each apostle within the network would "go their own way" with their sons and daughters, much like the early apostles did after they left Jerusalem.[47] Concerning his leadership, Simpson stated, "Sumrall built roads before there were paths to follow. Now our responsibility is to extend those roads."[48] It would be Lipscomb who would enlarge the network and understood Simpson's remarks as a prophetic declaration for the future of CFN.

In June of 2013, during the national conference of CFN, Lipscomb advanced a huge change in the paradigm of CFN. This shift was that CFN was to be a "movement of planting churches."[49] Up until this time, all church planting was to be left to the local churches of the various ministerial cells. Consequently, not much church planting had occurred. Lipscomb maintained that CFN was to continue "being a family," but now he declared that the Lord's direction was for CFN to be a church planting movement.

His theological foundation for this shift was *"missio Dei."* This is a Latin term that means "the mission of God" or "the sending of God." Lipscomb held that this mandate was not simply an activity, but rather that the mission is an attribute of God. As such, it was embedded in one's salvation. Moreover, he believed that the emphasis upon pastor and teacher, instead of the fivefold ministries, had limited this most important characteristic of God's nature. While we may not all be apostles, Lipscomb stated that we were all apostolic. Furthermore, the charismatic movement/revival was used by God for the purpose of waking each of us up to the mission of God for our lives. In fact, Lipscomb believed that the baptism of the Holy Spirit and the gifts of the Spirit were not the end but the means to becoming a missional movement.[50]

To advance this new direction, Lipscomb started "Mission 20/20." Lipscomb's desire for CFN was to start twenty new churches and twenty new networks by the year 2020. Under his leadership, CFN will start Activate

---

47. Sumrall, *Apostolic Fathers and Their Families*, 74.
48. Simpson, eulogy at Sumrall's funeral at Liberty Church, Pensacola, FL, January 16, 2013.
49. Lipscomb, "Road Ahead."
50. Ibid.

Internship Academy (AIA). This will be a school to train those who desire to plant a church.[51] Moreover, Lipscomb suggested that each network/ministerial cell develop its own AIA.[52] Howbeit, he was keenly aware that one cannot make a disciple in the classroom or on Sunday morning. Also, Lipscomb stated that the problem with one-on-one relational discipleship was that one made another like himself instead of a follower of Jesus. Discipleship should be done with a group that was endeavoring to be missional.[53]

Lipscomb was concerned that CFN needed to be centered upon mission. While relationships and a family atmosphere would continue, if one was not careful, then the idea of family could develop into an emphasis that would be too inward. For Lipscomb, the primary values for CFN needed to be relationships, resourcing, and reproductions. CFN was to move from being man centered (i.e., the apostle only) to being mission centered. To put it another way, Lipscomb stated that CFN was moving from being person centered to being principle centered.[54] For example, submission was not to be understood in terms of submitting only to one's leader/apostle; it was also to be understood in terms of mission, i.e., "sub-mission—to come under mission." For Lipscomb, apostolic meant missional.[55]

Lipscomb's Essentials for CFN

Lipscomb was convinced that CFN was to be a movement. He stated that the picture of what the Lord was directing in CFN would best be seen in Ezekiel 37—the valley of dry bones. By the various bones coming together, the Lord desired CFN to rise up as an army. Thereby, the movement would encompass the entire body and be an organic movement from the bottom up.[56] Lipscomb understood that for CFN to become an apostolic/missional movement several essentials were needed. He said that everything within this movement had to do with the Spirit of God, the transformative power of the gospel, and the central element for the ecclesia of "Jesus is Lord." Christology must be the theological touchstone of the movement. The massive theological weight loaded into these three words represented a whole worldview. It encom-

51. Ibid.
52. Lipscomb, "Re-Invisioning CFN."
53. Lipscomb, "Road Ahead."
54. Ibid.
55. Lipscomb, "Re-Invisioning CFN."
56. Lipscomb, "Road Ahead."

passed the aspect of leadership or sovereignty. It underscored the concept of relationship as God claims exclusive loyalty over his people. It admitted no idolatry for the ecclesia from the myriad of idols in all cultures—money, sex, power, ideology, or anything that demands loyalty that should belong to God. Moreover, the phrase captured the certainty that *Jesus* is the Lord. Change the name and the whole character of lordship would change accordingly.[57] If the church lost its defining contact with Jesus, then would lose the central focus of Christianity.[58] For Lipscomb, the lordship of Jesus was both the center and the circumference of the apostolic movement.

The second essential for CFN's future was that of discipleship and discipleship making. Discipleship, for Lipscomb, involved the life-long adventure of becoming like Jesus. Akin to the concept of apprenticeship, it expressed itself in a commitment to be like Christ, to live like him, and to rightly represent him in the culture. Lipscomb believed that movements only grow in proportion to their capacity to make disciples. Lipscomb stated that discipleship is how one lived out the lordship of Jesus.[59] Alan Hirsch called discipleship the process of "embodying the message," which was the basis of one's spiritual authority.[60] Hence Lipscomb understood leadership as directly proportional to discipleship, and as such discipleship was a key to cultivating an apostolic, missional ethos.

The third dictum that Lipscomb perceived for CFN was what he called "incarnational." Missionally speaking, it meant making Jesus real and not religious. He linked his point back to the fourth century and the time of Constantine.[61] Positively, with the church no longer facing extreme persecution, the great fathers of the church focused on developing the church's understanding of the great doctrines of the faith. Negatively, with mass conversions taking placing, it inevitably detracted from the depth of conviction and the moral life of the church. Moreover, with imperial protection the church came under the influence of imperial condemnation or favor, which gave theological controversies a political dimension they had not

---

57. This emphasis on Christology, for Lipscomb, is how the reality of the Trinity comes into focus—through the lens of the life and ministry of Jesus. One's identity is related to one's understanding and experience of Christ. But it is the Spirit, who is given to the church, that leads one into an understanding in Christ.

58. See Hirsch and Frost, *ReJesus*. Hirsch was one of Lipscomb's favorite authors.

59. Lipscomb, "Road Ahead."

60. Hirsch, *Forgotten Ways*, 114–16.

61. Lipscomb, "Road Ahead."

previously had.⁶² Because of the church's need to deal with the various heresies in that century, the church detached from its catalytic impulse on the mission of God—*missio Dei*. Conversely, Christianity was not united with the government, but if you were an American (with the exception of the last thirty years) you were a Christian. Our mentality became, "Come to us instead of go to them."⁶³ The apostolic, missional emphasis had become a subset of ecclesiology, rather than its passion. It was downgraded to an inferior function of the church and mainly concerned with overseas outreach.

Hence, if the church was to take its "sentness" seriously, then the way it was sent must be influenced by how God engaged the world in Jesus. Through the incarnation, God entered the world and loved people as an insider; he met people where they were. For Lipscomb, the apostolic movement, and especially CFN, must extend itself into the surrounding culture. If CFN was to be a movement, then at its epicenter must be an ongoing impulse to partner with God by creating an internal pressure outward into mission and downward into cultural incarnational engagement.⁶⁴

Lipscomb understood the fourth essential for CFN as apostolic culture. It was paramount in his understanding to broaden the understanding of ministry. The pastor/teacher framework often excluded more generative forms of leadership. Eph 4:11–12 offered critical genetic information concerning the ministry of the church. While we are not all apostles, we are all apostolic.⁶⁵ While oversight and accountability was necessary in the ministry, the fivefold gifting related to all the people in the church and not just those who lead. The Eph 4:11–12 paradigm concerned ministry and not necessarily leadership. Leadership was implied in ministry, but for Lipscomb everyone gets to participate.⁶⁶ Lipscomb desired to call into question the limited views handed down from institutional and missional neutered forms of ministry advanced by maintenance-minded churches and leaders.

The fifth crucial element for CFN to maintain its movement was its organic structure. One of the mainstays of Sumrall that Lipscomb embraced was a decentralized governmental structure. Moreover, Lipscomb

62. González, *History of Christian Thought*, 1:268–69. Also see Kelly, *Early Christian Doctrines*, 5–6.

63. Lipscomb, "Road Ahead."

64. See Cole, *Church 3.0*, and Friesen, *Thy Kingdom Connected*.

65. Lipscomb, "Road Ahead."

66. Hirsch, *Forgotten Ways*, 149–78.

Leadership and Directional Changes

believed that the church must function as an organism. He stated that when something is healthy it grows.[67] But the problem with an overly institutional church conception was that it tended to stagnate over time. What CFN needed was to reboot as a people movement. Lipscomb desired that CFN, as an apostolic movement, would avoid the centralization of power and instead would mobilize the people of God to become reproducing disciples within a structured network. One of the most potent doctrines of the church was the priesthood of all believers. CFN would be a movement where this axiom was lived out. As such, CFN would be able to achieve what Roland Allen called "spontaneous expansion."[68] Reproduction required reproducibility, which needed an ecclesiology simple enough for believers to reproduce. An example of church as an organism and a people movement was in China. With millions of adherents, the church there has grown without centralized headquarters, vast payrolls, buildings, etc. They simply spread from person to person.

Lipscomb described the last essential for CFN as *communitas*. *Communitas* is a Latin term that described an unstructured community where individuals were equal. It inferred an intense community spirit—a feeling of great social equality, solidarity, and togetherness. Popularized by Victor Turner, an anthropologist, it's defined as the interplay between structure and anti-structure. This coaction was characteristic of people experiencing liminality together. In the context of the apostolic network movement, liminality meant that which happens during times of transition that created a fluid, malleable situation that enabled a new direction and customs to become established. *Communitas*, thereby, was that piercing point of community that allowed the entire community to share a common experience. More pointedly, it was the personal experience of togetherness that occurred amidst a countercultural circumstance. Turner stated that it was an absolute interhuman relation beyond any form of structure.[69] Lipscomb learned this concept from Allen Hirsch,[70] an author who made a profound impact upon him.

---

67. Lipscomb, "Road Ahead."

68. Allan, *Spontaneous Expansion of the Church*, 143–58.

69. Tuner, *Dramas, Fields, and Metaphors*, 231–71, 274; Tuner, *Revelation and Divination in Ndembu Ritual*, 21–22; Tuner and Turner, *Image and Pilgrimage in Christian Culture*, 250–55. Also see Turner, *Ritual Process*.

70. Hirsch, *Forgotten Ways*, 217–42.

Lipscomb ascertained that *communitas* was present in every major people movement, especially religious movements. For him, it was where the community of faith centered around, or upon a very serious purpose. As such, they developed a shared drive or passion that prioritized their lives and commitments. People changed from being companions to being comrades, from being associates to being partners who were bound together in a common cause. Hence, believers would move from being safe and predictable into an open-ended learning experience by networking with others in the kingdom of God, especially through church planting.[71]

These six essentials were the backbone of what Lipscomb understood of the new direction for CFN and its theological foundation of *missio Dei*. They were much more than a methodology; they were his mindset on "how to be church." It wasn't just a matter of thinking one's way into a new way of acting, but acting one's way into a new way of thinking.

Summary

With the death of Ken Sumrall, CFN came under the influence of his successors, L. A. Joiner and Buford Lipscomb. Both men were passionate about their convictions. Joiner's beliefs grew to include the discipleship principles of the Shepherding Movement. He identified with Simpson's emphasis upon the local church and godly authority governing it. During his tenure as head apostle (some referred to this position as "executive director"), he continued Sumrall's position of CFN being a decentralized network. The local church was primary, as well as the need for godly relationships. Apostles would continue to serve as the spiritual fathers to all who would relate to them. The apostle's job was to encourage them and help the local churches during times of difficulties.

Lipscomb, on the other hand, moved CFN toward a more missional paradigm. No longer would it be a person-centered network but a principle-centered one. He opened up the opportunity for any CFN church to voluntarily contribute funds to help with the new church planting paradigm.[72] Hence, while he does not believe in a centralized government, he does believe in centralized resources.[73] Joiner did not. For him, everything was in the hands of the local church. During his tenure, Lipscomb has been

71. Lipscomb, "Road Ahead."
72. Lipscomb, "Re-Invisioning CFN."
73. Kelly, interview with author, May 20, 2012.

much more inclusive and has done much more networking with other groups, be they denominations or not. His outlook is global. Joiner's views were more concerned with the issues of CFN.[74]

Lipscomb's timeline for many of the changes for CFN begins in January 2014. Time will tell if the ministerial cells of CFN will partner with his vision or, as Sumrall stated, if each cell will "go their own way."

---

74. Mather, interview with author, March 1, 2012.

9

Reflections

THE MODERN-DAY APOSTOLIC NETWORK movement has been developing over several decades. With its roots going back to the early 1800s through the leadership of Edward Irving and the Catholic Apostolic Church to the Latter Rain Movement of the 1940s, the idea of modern apostles continued to develop. Much has changed since that time, but the concept of apostles has not died out. Church Foundational Network has provided a fresh link with this rich historical past. Since its inception much has changed, and the scope of time has allowed for a more discernible reflection of CFN. As such, several observations can be suggested.

Historical Observations

Church Foundational Network was birthed as a renewal movement whose theological inspiration was driven by a restorational idealism. As a movement, it sought to rediscover some elements that the modern church was missing—a more biblically based governmental structure.[1] Ken Sumrall and L. A. Joiner understood that their commissioning was to restore the fivefold ministry paradigm of Eph 4:11–12. Motivated by a non-cessationist axiom, they taught the restoration of apostolic government.

Moreover, renewal movements have been perceived as a threat to established status quo, and resisted by existing church structures with judgment or criticism. Hence, strife and strain accompanied CFN's break with Liberty Fellowship of Ministers and Churches. CFN challenged the non-relational structure of LFMC and its centralized control over its constituents.

---

1. Snyder, *Signs of the Spirit*, 269. Snyder points out renewal movements generally "rediscover some element in the church or Scripture."

Reflections

Without question, Sumrall was driven to see apostolic networks challenge the deteriorating structures of denominationalism. Believing that God's best structure for the church was a theocracy, restoring the role of the modern-day apostle was paramount for him. His restorationism was energized by his eschatological outlook that restoring church government around apostles as spiritual fathers of leaders was part of God's end-time plan.[2]

Second, CFN became a local-church-centered movement and network. Sumrall believed in developing a network of local ministers and churches that operated in freedom from denominational control. With the emphasis upon the apostle and his apostolic council, CFN focused upon building a relational based network of churches and leaders. Far from seeing themselves as exclusivist, they were open to any group that held similar views.

Third, CFN felt that the contemporary church structures of denominations were inadequate, especially in the area of congregational government. The local church was paramount, and each ministerial cell within CFN served to encourage their growth and provide oversight when needed. Much as in pietism and the house groups of early nineteenth-century Methodism, CFN's building block was connecting the various ministerial cells and thereby establishing a relationally based network of churches. Sumrall saw this as the answer to the cry for spiritual fathers and the impersonal church structure based on geographical location.

Fourth, while the main thrust of CFN was the local church, pastoral care came from the relationship with one's spiritual father/apostle. Nothing was more paramount to its ethos than this belief. The importance of this relational base for apostolic oversight was affirmed throughout the tenures of both Sumrall and Joiner.

Fifth, CFN was a network whose authority structure was hierarchical. It was not hierarchical as in the classical system of denominational church government, but it was in the sense that the ministerial cell involved a top-down approach to the exercise of authority. Sumrall underscored that each member of CFN volunteered to be held accountable to his spiritual father/apostle, and his council and could remove themselves from that accountability upon request.[3] Also, submission meant subordination to an office or to a person and did not require unquestioning obedience.[4] The

---

2. Sumrall, *New Wine Bottles*, 33–40.
3. Sumrall, *Apostolic Fathers and Their Families*, 92.
4. Ibid., 31–32.

apostolic council was in place to confirm the direction of its members, not give permission.[5]

Last of all, CFN saw the church as being relational and organic in its nature. It supported and valued the "joints" of individuals connecting within the ministerial cells, and the ministerial cells connecting with other cells and networks. These relationships were both long term and short term, depending on the purpose of the relating. Hence it highlighted its interdependence and mutuality.

The Influence of Simpson

The radical call of the Shepherding Movement was to bring the local church and local believer into maturity by intense discipleship. Thereby the kingdom of God would be advanced. While there were harmful results from the Shepherding Movement, its influence continued to be felt. For example, the cell/home-base church models continue to be used in many denominations today.[6] Moreover, C. Peter Wagner and others sought to analyze the ecclesiological shifts of the modern-day apostolic network movement by their tendencies to emphasis personal relationships. Many of their observations were similar to the Shepherding Movement.[7] Indeed the teachings of the Shepherding Movement of the 1970s and 1980s and Sumrall's friendship with Simpson revealed very similar positions that CFN has embraced.

Both Sumrall and Simpson agreed upon the need for a plurality of elders, but maintained the principle of headship in which a single leader had the final authority.[8] Convinced that the Spirit was restoring the church to maturity, they both emphasized the restoration of the fivefold ministries of apostle, prophet, evangelist, shepherd (i.e., pastor), and teacher. For Simpson God was re-establishing authority in the church, and for Sumrall God was restoring New Testament governmental structure to the church.[9]

5. Sumrall, *New Wine Bottles*, 116–17.

6. See Stockstill, *Cell Church*; Beckham, *Second Reformation*; and Neighbor, *Where Do We Go From Here?*, just to name a few books on this subject.

7. George, *Coming Church Revolution*; George, *Preparing Your Church for the Future*; Giles, *What on Earth Is the Church?*; Wagner, *New Apostolic Churches*; Wagner, *Churchquake*. Also it should be pointed out that much of the principles of the men's movement Promise Keepers hold some of the same ideals as the Shepherding Movement.

8. Prince, "Local Church," 14–18; Sumrall, *Apostolic Fathers and Their Families*, 20–22.

9. Baxter, *Thy Kingdom Come*, 16; Sumrall, *Apostolic Fathers and Their Families*,

Additionally, both advanced the restoration of spiritual fatherhood. The goal was to establish a nurturing relationship with one's spiritual authority. Believers were encouraged to discover fatherhood in their shepherd.[10] Sumrall, who was known as "Papa Ken," understood each apostle within the ministerial cells of CFN as a spiritual father.[11] It should be pointed out that many within the Shepherding Movement understood the five leaders as apostles, though the leaders never referred to themselves as apostles.[12] Additionally, the governmental concept of a tribe was integral in their thinking. At the beginning of CFN, Sumrall discerned the tribe concept of church government, but in the end he settled for the concepts of a "family of ministers" and fatherhood.[13] The five leaders in the Shepherding Movement had maintained their own independent structures. To facilitate these formats they used the biblical picture of Israel's tribes. Ultimately, Simpson opted for and promoted the concept of "one nation." After the Shepherding Movement dissolved, in 1987 Simpson started a network of churches and ministries called the Fellowship of Covenant Ministers and Churches. FCMC carried on the central themes of the Shepherding Movement of covenant relationships with God and other believers.[14] Howbeit, Simpson had realized that the extra-local authority of the movement had created a type of pyramidal leadership structure that bonded people into relationships. If these relationships with one's shepherd were broken, then Simpson understood that the believer's relationship with the local church broke down as well as local churches' relationship with other churches. Simpson changed his position to simply encouraging relationships with other leaders, i.e., the pastor, but not with the church as a whole.[15] By 1993 Simpson decided to dissolve FCMC, but he continued to pastor leaders. Some of these individuals were leaders of large networks of churches.[16] It was this paradigm that

---

19–25. For the Shepherding Movement, the key leader was the shepherd, but for CFN the key leader was the apostle.

10. Bob Mumford, "Disciple Position Paper," unpublished paper, 1976, as quoted in Moore, *Shepherding Movement*, 77–78.

11. Sumrall, *Apostolic Fathers and Their Families*, 59–66.

12. Simpson, interview with author, March 9, 2012.

13. Sumrall, *Practical Church Government*, 41–57, and Sumrall, *Apostolic Fathers and Their Families*, 7.

14. Moore, *Shepherding Movement*, 176–77.

15. Simpson, *Challenge to Care*.

16. Joiner now relates to Simpson as his pastor, or as he puts it, "his elder brother." Joiner, email message to author, September 24, 2013.

Simpson brought into his renewed relationship with Sumrall. At the birthing of CFN, Sumrall used Simpson's outline that he preached at Liberty Fellowship's annual conference.[17] Both Sumrall and Simpson believed in and taught a need to restore the church to a more New Testament pattern and advanced an ecclesiology that was based on apostolic networks.

The Devil Is in the Details

Sumrall taught and believed that CFN would embody Mal 4:5–6: "Behold, I will send you Elijah the prophet before the coming of the great and dreadful day of the Lord. And he will turn the hearts of the fathers to the children, and the hearts of the children to their fathers, lest I come and strike the earth with a curse." Sumrall understood that the Spirit was preparing ministers in the last days for a great harvest before the coming of the Lord. While the early church experienced an outpouring of the Spirit, so the "last church" would experience an even greater cascade. He revealed his charismatic passion by stating, "As the church was birthed in Holy Ghost fire, so the last church will experience an even greater flame that will cleanse, refine and melt hearts together in holy love."[18]

To gird the church for this great outpouring, Sumrall postulated several key issues. First, there would be a Spirit-created hunger in the souls of his saints. Second, the Spirit would establish a desire in "fathers" to turn their hearts to their "sons and daughters." This move would not be localized and would include both natural and spiritual families. Third, God would anoint certain men (i.e., apostles) to raise up ministerial sons and daughters who would, in turn, raise up their own spiritual families. Fourth, he stated that the church would begin to hunger for this new apostolic movement. Last, the Spirit would raise up a new wine skin to govern this last-day outpouring.[19] Developing a relationship with one's spiritual father was paramount in both Sumrall's and Joiner's thinking.

In implementing this relational dynamic in CFN's governing paradigm, concerns began to surface. For example, some ministerial cells were quite large. How many father-son or father-daughter relationships could one apostle effectively maintain? Moreover, how could an apostle cultivate an effective relationship with the churches under his oversight? How should

17. Sumrall, *Apostolic Fathers and Their Families*, 9–10.
18. Ibid., iv.
19. Ibid., iv–v.

Reflections

one define that? What would it look like? John Carney, a CFN apostolic father in Salem, Oregon, offered this insight:

> I find that the difficulty with apostolic involvement in the local church is the absence of pre-existing agreements that lay out a process. As you and all the men know from experience, when you are to intervene in a difficult situation there are often not clear guide lines in place, which gives place for everyone to start reacting. . . . I am finding that apostolic relationship with the pastor or elders is not enough. There must be viable relations with the congregation to the point that they know that the apostolic leader knows and values the ministries, spiritual DNA and expressions which make them who they are as a fellowship.[20]

Even if an apostolic leader could meet with the congregations under his oversight several times a year, would that allow for a governing relationship to truly exist?

Joiner, on the other hand, discerned a different issue within governmental relationships. Within his ministerial cell, Christian Alliance of Ministers (CAM), elders in the local churches were deferring to his counsel for their local situations and troubles. He began to feel like he was acting as a denomination head of sorts. His strong belief was that the local church should be able to minister to itself, support itself, and govern itself. He felt that at times his oversight of churches interfered or weakened the local church.[21] The network leaders had underestimated the codependent dynamic in many people.

Consequently, in November of 2012 Joiner made an amendment to the Christian Alliance of Ministries manual. Under the section entitled "The Apostle and the Local Church," the apostle's involvement in the local church was made clear:

> The Apostle shall serve the local church as General Overseer. If the Senior Pastor and leadership team recognize the Apostle as the Apostle/Overseer of that local assembly, the Apostle/Overseer shall assume the role as Pastor to the pastor and Overseer of the church. This trans-local leadership function will be one born out of relationship and should not be seen solely as a political role. As Overseer, the Apostle will meet with the leadership team at

---

20 Carney, quoted in Sumrall, *Apostolic Fathers and Their Families*, 89.

21. Many of the elders in the local churches would not make church policies or decisions without Joiner's input or approval. Joiner, interview with author, November 30, 2012.

least once per year and speak to the congregation as invited by the Senior Pastor. This is an important function as it helps to build a relationship with the congregation so that there is a connection to the church in times of need. The Overseer shall serve the church leadership in assisting them in filling vacancies in leadership positions. The Apostle/Overseer shall serve in other ways as defined in this Faith and Practice.[22]

Joiner came to believe that he had allowed CAM to get involved in church oversight in a way that was beyond God's original intent. The new language of this section stated:

> The Apostle shall serve as pastor to the senior pastor of the local church. Pastoral oversight of the pastor, including but not limited to counseling, encouraging, accountability, etc., should not be seen as an official oversight of the church itself. This relationship will be purely a voluntary connection on the part of both the senior pastor and the apostle.
>
> In the event that the church leadership, led by the Senior Pastor or Senior Leader of the church asks for counsel from the apostle, the apostle will then consider the request. He then may render counsel, but his counsel is not to be seen as a mandatory ruling, meaning the decision is to be indigenous to the local church leaders.
>
> If the office of Senior Pastor of a church is vacated and the leadership team contacts the lead apostle of CAM for assistance, any advice offered at this time is only given to assist the local elders of the church in making the decisions necessary to fill the vacancy.[23]

With this amendment, Joiner stated that he would pastor men but not oversee churches. His relationship with the senior leaders would be strictly voluntary and based on relationship with them. Consequently, Joiner severely limited any "extra-local" authority with the churches in CAM and under his apostolic oversight.[24] In fact, his views were akin to Simpson's posi-

---

22. Joiner, letter to Christian Alliance of Ministries Family, November 3, 2012, private holding.

23. Ibid.

24. Sumrall, *Apostolic Fathers and Their Families*, 27. With this decision, Joiner began moving away from CFN's original position. Sumrall stated that "trans-local authority and ministry is that which extends beyond a local church. The churches written to and about in the New Testament were not independent and autonomous with local elders or the congregation acting independently of any outside oversight."

tion. Simpson understood modern-day apostles as having more authority in churches they have planted. But having extra-local authority over all churches within their ministerial cells would be something that Simpson would not embrace. For him and Joiner, such a position would be seen as that of a "bishop," and that was too denominational.[25]

These examples underscored the need for structuring the various relationships throughout the CFN network. Implementing how the various relationships function revealed a need for boundaries. In any relationship, oftentimes the devil is in the details!

Changes in the Wind

While Sumrall was still alive, Lipscomb continued CFN direction out of honor for him. But during that time Lipscomb started connecting with other apostolic network leaders and learning from their approach to ministry. With Sumrall's death, Lipscomb moved within months to make major changes to CFN.

First, Lipscomb shifted the emphasis of CFN from being individual centered (i.e., focus upon the apostle and his counsel) to being mission centered, that is, from being person centered to being principle centered. During their tenure of leading the network, both Sumrall and Joiner maintained the primacy of apostles as spiritual fathers to their sons and daughters. The leadership structure was primarily an oligarchy, with each individual ministerial cell having authority to make policy. The advantage from this governmental structure was that decisions could be made swiftly while allowing the vision to remain focused. For CFN, the vision was to be a decentralized network of churches, to identify and relate with leaders for equipping others, and to promote apostolic ministry and oversight for the people of God.[26] Lipscomb, while still maintaining CFN's decentralized structure, changed the primary vision to planting churches and adding new networks. He repositioned the emphasis to Article IV, Sections 3 and 4, of the Articles of Incorporation. These sections stated, "To unite its ministers and churches for effective promotion of the Kingdom of God (Ephesians 4:1–16). To share responsibility in fulfilling the Great Commission of

---

25. Simpson, interview with author, March 9, 2012.
26. Sumrall, *Apostolic Fathers and Their Families*, 96–97.

Christ: i.e., the proclamation of the Gospel of the Kingdom and evangelization of the world."[27]

To accomplish this task, Lipscomb developed a system of voluntary giving for all ministers and churches within CFN. The suggestion has been made that each affiliated church or ministerial cells should contribute 2 percent of their gross income. It should be pointed out that the principle of "tithing up" to one's apostolic council was not replace by Lipscomb.[28] Some, however, had concerns that the concept of spiritual fathering would fall by the wayside in this new direction. Others had apprehensions that Lipscomb was moving towards a centralized governing structure, and thereby a denomination. Lipscomb's position was simply that CFN was providing opportunity to create synergy by pooling resources for the purpose of fulfilling the Great Commission.[29]

Lipscomb's leadership has taken the emphasis of CFN off the local church and changed it in an apostolic, missional direction. His paradigm is global. In fact, the main difference between Sumrall, Joiner, and Lipscomb is that Lipscomb has been much more inclusive, especially from the fact that he has reached out to other networks that are unlike CFN.[30] Joiner never saw his tenure as the head of CFN as strategic. As such, he did not develop any vital long-term vision for the growth of the network.[31]

Through these changes Lipscomb has, for practical purposes, changed CFN from being a network of independent ministerial cells and churches to a federation of churches. This federation is built around the sodality of apostolic missions. While there is no centralized headquarters for CFN and each ministerial cell still remains autonomous, Liberty Church of Pensacola, Florida, is understood as the mother church for the network.[32] In the end, Lipscomb has taught that CFN is to be a decentralized governmental network of ministries that shares centralized resources.[33] Some have seen this as the beginning of a denomination; others have understood it as creating cooperation for kingdom advancement.

27. Church Foundational Network, "Articles of Incorporation," article IV, "Purpose and Functions of the Network."
28. Lipscomb, "Re-Invisioning CFN."
29. Lipscomb, interview with author, April 18, 2013.
30. Mather, interview with author, March 1, 2012.
31. Limbaugh, interview with author, March 8, 2012.
32. Lipscomb, "Re-Invisioning CFN."
33. Kelly, interview with author, May 17, 2012.

Reflections

Charismatic Roots

Sumrall was a major leader in the charismatic movement of the 1960s and 1970s. He firmly believed in the baptism of the Holy Spirit and in the need for the gifts of the Spirit for the believer. In 1994, Sumrall stated the following:

> Men were created to have fellowship with God who is Spirit; therefore they have a void in their life for the supernatural. If this void is not filled with the supernatural power of God, it will be filled by the evil one. Christianity was supernatural from its very first day, and it will be supernatural until the last. The Lord gave His church supernatural power to be witness of His resurrection, and the world will require no less to really believe it.[34]

Additionally, the charter for CFN confirmed Sumrall's charismatic convictions. Under Article VII, Section 14, entitled "Holy Spirit," Sumrall stated, "We believe that the manifestation of the Holy Spirit, recorded in 1 Corinthians 12:8–11, shall operate in present-day churches which yield to the Lord Jesus Christ. . . . We believe that the Baptism of the Holy Spirit is for all believers as promised by John the Baptist and was witnessed by the early disciples of Jesus Christ."[35] However, the section concludes with a qualifying remark set off in parentheses: "it is not necessary that all cells believe alike as to the evidence of receiving the Baptism in the Holy Spirit. Each cell leaders and his council may determine what to place in the cell charter regarding this matter."[36]

Sumrall's intentions were to create an environment where diversity would be welcomed. Since 1995, CFN has developed into a great mix of ideas and opinions from its ministerial cells.[37] As such, it has various theological views and philosophies of ministry. Lipscomb has continued to support this diversity. During his tenure, Sumrall would have mostly his cell ministers speak at the conferences. Lipscomb, on the other hand, would involve other ministers who held different philosophies of ministry. Some of these ministers would not be considered charismatic or Pentecostal.[38]

---

34. Sumrall, *Confidence*, 59.
35. Church Foundational Network, "Articles of Incorporation," article VII, "Articles of Faith."
36. Ibid.
37. Limbaugh, interview with author, March 15, 2012.
38. Mather, interview with author, March 15, 2012.

The primary reason behind Lipscomb's direction came from his understanding of the future of the charismatic movement. He stated that the movement accomplished what God desired, i.e., to bring back the Holy Spirit and his gifts to believers and to the local church. Moreover, the charismatic movement was instrumental in restoring the fivefold ministry. Now the movement was part of the whole. It would be just as valid as it has always been, but God was moving his church in another direction. Lipscomb believed that the movement was coming together around the kingdom of God, especially the apostolic/missional dimensions. He reflected a Keswick viewpoint because he understood the power of the Holy Spirit as the means to carry out the gospel of the kingdom. The charismatic capacity was now maturing within the newer apostolic network movement.[39]

Others on the CFN council agreed with Lipscomb. For example, Charles Simpson stated that if you don't see the gifts in the church and through the church, then that church does not qualify as charismatic. Being focused upon the baptism of the Holy Spirit and the gifts of the Spirit was what defined the charismatic movement. If the church did not have a place for them to function, then it was no longer a charismatic fellowship. However, Simpson understood that the decline in the movement was because people were no longer attracted to the gifts. He admitted that sometimes the gifts were not authentic.[40] Also, Ron Kelly and Joiner, both key leaders within the network, agreed that the church was in a post-charismatic era.[41] Both posited that the baptism of the Holy Spirit was for empowerment for effective ministry—a Keswick position.[42]

This history of CFN reveals that the network has moved beyond its original charismatic foundation. Today the main emphasis of the majority of its churches has been developing an apostolic/missional people. The gifts

---

39. Lipscomb, interview with author, April 20, 2013. Lipscomb stated that aspects of the CM being a revival or renewal are not over. His emphasis is upon how the gifts work within the apostolic/missional paradigm. At the June 2013 CFN conference Lipscomb stated, "We believe in the gifts of the Spirit operating in believers and in the church. However, we just don't want it to be 'weird.'" Lipscomb, "Road Ahead."

40. Simpson, interview with author, March 15, 2012. Simpson also stated, "I pursue the Spirit. But I don't measure what I am doing by manifestations. If there is a manifestation called for, then that's fine."

41. Kelly, interview with author, May 17, 2012; Joiner, interview with author, February 12, 2012.

42. Dayton, *Theological Roots of Pentecostalism*, 95–108; Synan, *Holiness-Pentecostal Tradition*, 143–45.

of the Spirit were not rejected but seen as tools to make one effective in the harvest of souls for the kingdom of God.

Conclusion

History has chronicled the latent stress in renewal movements between the charismatic restorationism and institutionalism. This account has recorded CFN's striking growth as a renewal movement. All three leaders of CFN embraced and maintained a paradigm that church government should be decentralized and relational. They had experienced their own battles with institutional Christianity and came to believe that the Holy Spirit was restoring a more New Testament pattern for governing God's people. They maintained throughout the years that CFN was an organic association of ministries.

Both Sumrall and Joiner kept their focus on the local church, building relationships, and equipping leaders. However, when Lipscomb took the helm of leadership changes were forthcoming. Shifting away from a person-centered paradigm to a mission-centered, church-planting model, Lipscomb had to deal with the inexorable force of institutionalization: the necessity for order, resourcing, communication, and continuation. Through his changes, Lipscomb revealed the lesson of history that radical renewal movements tend to moderate and accommodate over time. Howbeit Lipscomb's focus was and continues to be global. His strategic vision for twenty new churches and twenty new networks required the need for adjustment.

It is clear that Sumrall's vision for an apostolic government of "spiritual fathers" was at least a harbinger. While both Sumrall and Joiner concentrated on the office gift of apostle, Lipscomb addressed a deeper ecclesiological issue—releasing an apostolic people.

Appendix

THE HISTORY OF CHURCH Foundational Network (CFN) has revealed the evolution of changes that were created at its birth. At its genesis in 1995, changes occurred not just to CFN but also to Liberty Fellowship of Ministers and Churches (LFMC). Additionally, with the changing of leadership from Sumrall to Joiner and finally to Lipscomb, CFN has grown but created new issues that are at odds with its earlier vision and paradigm. However, with these concerns new opportunities have been discussed. The following is a closer look at those changes.

Liberty Fellowship of Ministers and Churches

In January of 1995, LFMC was a growing fellowship with a total membership of 352 individuals. Later that year, Sumrall maintained that 22 ministers followed him from LFMC to start CFN. But the affect upon LFMC was much more severe. A total of 93 ministers left LFMC. Twenty-two went with CFN, and 71 left the fellowship and did not join with CFN as they disapproved with either how the decision was made to begin CFN or the way in which the decision was handled.[1] Since that time, LFMC has seen a 56-percent drop in its membership. The following table outlines the downward spiral of LFMC since 2001.[2]

---

1. All the individuals who were interviewed stated that the meetings concerning birthing CFN were very heated.

2. Barch, email to author, October 23, 2013. Mrs. Barch is the executive office secretary for LFMC. Presently, the LFMC office is located in Arlington, Texas.

Appendix

Year	Membership[3]
2000–2001	150
2001–2002	167
2002–2003	159
2003–2004	157
2004–2005	45
2005–2006	160
2006–2007	170
2007–2008	148
2008–2009	139
2009–2010	136
2010–2011	117
2011–2012	113
2012–2013	115

These numbers were taken from printed rosters and excel rosters of LFMC. While LFMC has maintained a positive outlook, these numbers reveal a troubling picture for its future.[3]

However, LFMC has planted at least two churches during the decline. In September of 2008, Bridge Builder Community Church was planted by Tim and Ginny Millard in Hyde Park, New York. Then in July of 2010, Bay Shore Community Church of Millsboro, Delaware, an existing member of LFMC, planted a satellite campus church in Rehoboth Beach, Delaware. Danny Tice is the lead pastor and Matt Krimm is the campus pastor.[4]

Moreover, LFMC has undergone some significant shifts in its philosophy of ministry. One such change is its shift toward committed relationships. On their website, LFMC makes the following statement:

> Liberty Fellowship desires to provide a platform of authentic, God honoring relationships that are open, honest and helpful. We consider this to be one of our strong points as a Fellowship.

---

3. Membership represents individual ministers. LFMC considered their churches to be part of the fellowship if the member was a pastor leading a church. Obviously these numbers do not reflect the membership of their churches. Also, some of its members were missionaries.

4. Liberty Fellowship, "Liberty Fellowship Church Plants," http://libertyfellowship.org/about/church-plants/.

Appendix

This is done through our annual family summer conference and our winter regional conferences. Beyond these conferences, Liberty Fellowship believes that each member must intentionally pursue relationships with other members. We understand that this requires a commitment of time, but feel strongly that pursuing meaningful relational connections is essential for all spiritual leaders. Security and stability are experienced in the context of trusting relationships.[5]

Such a commitment towards relationship was not prominent in its beliefs before 1995. In fact, in its "Core Values" section, the website states, "Pursuing meaningful relational connections is essential for all spiritual leaders, and we consider this one [sic] or our strong points as a Fellowship. Security and stability are experienced in the context of trusting relationships."[6] Moreover, the website's statement continues with relationship being the foundation for accountability: "Liberty Fellowship is a safe place to submit your life and ministry. Oversight within the Fellowship does not come from a desire to control, rather it flows from the desire for accountability and relationship from/with our members. Relational trust is the foundation upon which genuine authority and accountability can be most effectively exercised."[7] One major change that Liberty now allows is oversight by relationship. While its governmental structure is still divided into districts with an overseer over each one, they now allow ministers to choose an overseer in another district if they have a better relationship with that individual.[8] This is a significant shift towards CFN's understanding of apostolic oversight.

Also, LFMC, while maintaining its legal name, has shortened its name to Liberty Fellowship following the split with CFN. Notwithstanding, Liberty Fellowship sees itself as an apostolic network. Until the leadership of Lipscomb, the major difference between LFMC and CFN was that LFMC planted churches. Moreover, LFMC does not have a significant global presence.

---

5. Liberty Fellowship, "Fellowship," http://libertyfellowship.org/fellowship/.

6. Liberty Fellowship, "Liberty Core Value Statement," http://libertyfellowship.org/about/core-values/, para. 5.

7. Ibid.

8. Barch, telephone conversation with author, October 30, 2013.

Appendix

Church Foundational Network

Unlike LFCM, CFN has grown notably. Since 1995 to present, CFN has grown to over six hundred members. Additionally, CFN has a strong global presence through its members. For example, Ron and Pat Kelly are senior leaders for Living Waters International. LWI primarily ministers to orphan kids in both Guatemala and Albania. Through their Adopt-a-Kid programs, they presently minister to over ten thousand children a week by providing for their physical, medical, and spiritual needs. Also, the majority of their parents have come to know the Lord, and so LWI has planted multiple churches in these countries.[9] Ron and Pat are making plans to start an Adopt-a-Kid ministry in Egypt soon.

Sudip Khadka, a CFN ministerial cell leader, is actively involved in church planting, teaching, preaching, and sharing the redeeming power of the Lord in Nepal and its neighboring countries. Sudip and his wife, Lise, are actively involved in "planting churches and providing oversight and leadership to several churches in Nepal and in the neighbor country India. They hold evangelist crusades and leadership seminars. They are raising, equipping and training indigenous people and are sending them as missionaries to their own people through Compassion for Asia Bible College."[10]

With the new commitment of Lipscomb's 20/20 vision (twenty new churches and twenty new cells by the year 2020), more church plants are forthcoming both in the United States and abroad. Funds are presently being collected for this endeavor.

With the passage of time, CFN has undergone a change in its governmental structure, much like LFMC has changed. From its beginning, CFN was to be led by apostles who would each have their own ministerial cell. These apostles were considered to be "spiritual fathers" who underscored the importance of CFN's commitment to relational government. As long as Sumrall was alive, he was considered the senior apostle for CFN. He was affectionately known as "Papa Ken." Sumrall's apostolic council looked to him as their spiritual father, i.e., apostle. When he decided to step down, Sumrall appointed L. A. Joiner as his successor. Soon after Joiner's appointment, Sumrall's position of senior apostle was changed to "executive director." The primary reason for this shift was that, while Joiner was a great

---

9. Church Foundational Network, "Ron Kelly," http://www.cfnonline.org/ronkelly/.

10 Church Foundational Network, "Supid Khadra," http://www.cfnonline.org/sudipkhadka/.

replacement for Sumrall, many did not see him as their "spiritual father," i.e., their apostle.

Moreover, this scenario is repeating itself within the various ministerial cells. Each time a senior leader who is recognized as an apostle retires or dies, his "spiritual son" replaces him. Even though the individual is a good leader, many within the cell do not consider him their "spiritual father." As a result, he becomes the "executive director" for the cell. This represents a shift from Sumrall's original vision for CFN, and is evidence of routinization and institutionalism.

More positively, Lipscomb remains friends with many within Liberty Fellowship. In fact, he was the featured speaker at Liberty's annual conference in 2013. Many from Liberty Fellowship attended CFN's conference the same year. There is discussion concerning the possibility of both groups merging sometime in the future. But much would need to be worked out for this to become a reality. Time will tell.

Post-Charismatic Era

Every major leader within CFN admits that, as a movement, CFN is in a post-charismatic era. Jim Mather understands apostolic in such a way that allows mainline churches to embrace it. He adamantly teaches that all believers need the Holy Spirit, but his moving in the churches might not be called charismatic.[11] Ron Kelly believes that the charismatic movement became deluded by the waxing cold of believers. He is not sure we should go back to a charismatic methodology, but teach the baptism of the Holy Spirit as empowerment for effective ministry.[12] Marc Limbaugh no longer pushes the baptism of the Spirit or the gifts of the Spirit. He allows his members to seek this experience privately.[13] Buford Lipscomb takes a more holistic view. He believes that the charismatic movement accomplished what God desired: bringing back the Holy Spirit and his gifts to the believer and the church, and restoring the fivefold ministry. Now the charismatic dimension is part of the whole. It is just as valuable as it has always been, but now God is moving the church into a new direction, an apostolic/missional direction. Moreover, the power of the Holy Spirit is the means of carrying out the gospel of the kingdom. Today is just a different season for the church.

11. Mather, telephone interview with author, March 1, 2012.
12. Kelly, telephone interview with author, May 12, 2012.
13. Limbaugh, telephone interview with author, March 8, 2012.

For Lipscomb, the charismatic movement served its purpose and is now maturing within the apostolic network movement.[14]

Many who are sojourning in this post-charismatic era are exploring how to be charismatic in a theological and practice sense, without the extremes and abuses of the past. This is a common conviction of Lipscomb. He desires the charismatic dimension without being "weird." As an apostolic/missional network, he teaches a healthy focus on "being the church." Also, he teaches with a renewed interest in what Jesus meant by "the kingdom of God," which has quickly become his starting point for building missional *communitas*. This emphasis of Lipscomb is bring a healthy corrective to a "come to our event" mentality for more of a "get outside the four walls of the church, make friends, and bring the Kingdom with you" mentality.

Lipscomb's model seeks to break down the barrier between the sacred/secular divide in the church. He is convinced that as CFN embraces the apostolic/missional paradigm, new models for expressing the compassion of Christ and the presence of the Holy Spirit will emerge. This new direction for him is shifting CFN from a "homesteader" mentality to a "pioneer" one. The model must be adjusted to fit the message by taking into account changes that have occurred in culture. Lipscomb understands the importance of the interplay between the message, model, and market for CFN to be effective.[15]

For Lipscomb, the message of the kingdom of God is rooted in the biblical narrative and does not change over time. A shift away from an overt emphasis on the charismata and the baptism of the Holy Spirit occurred because the questions of the culture are inevitably different when compared to the beginning of the charismatic era of the 1960s and 1970s. Hence the model of "doing church" has been in flux. There is nothing sacred about one's dress, music type, or the physical structure in which one meets. It stands to reason that one's organizational structural would change with the times. Finally, the message and model will always respond to the market for Christianity, which is constantly changing as the culture changes.

Lipscomb seemed to instinctively know that too many charismatic churches were trying to apply 1960s models to the twenty-first-century church. While still believing in the need for the baptism of the Holy Spirit and the gifts of the Spirit, Lipscomb understood the need to communicate

---

14. Lipscomb, telephone interview with author, February 18, 2012.

15. I am indebted to Donald E. Miller for this concept. See Miller, "Routinizing Charisma."

the gospel in a way that culture would accept. One should always be trying to adjust the model to the market, and the message should respond to the questions being asked in the current context. In short, leaders within CFN should not only exegete Scripture, but culture as well.

Thereby, the model and message geared toward the baby boomers of the 1960s and 1970s will not meet the challenges of the millennialist generation today. For example, Lipscomb continues to underscore the relational aspect of CFN because he knows the culture is riddled with fractured families from which many adults come. The truth of Scripture must be both propositional and experiential. This experience will be lived out in the context of the community of believers.

Conclusion

Church Foundational Network represents a different genre for a religious organization. This new paradigm of independent churches is deeply suspicious of any denomination. In addition to its decentralized structure, CFN has pioneered a new governmental oversight based on the Eph 4:11–12 model. Unlike the Reformation led by Martin Luther, CFN has challenged not just doctrine but the medium through which the church is governed.

However, it is inevitable that charismatic leaders die. When this happens, the challenge is to understand how the movement will evolve. Will CFN hold on to the original vision that drew ministers to it, or as people age will it settle for structure and comfort? Lipscomb is determined that CFN will not only honor its past but launch into its apostolic/missional future. To do so, there are a few elements that will probably be needed. First, an emphasis on competence and character should be the foundation for maturing in the gifts of the Spirit. It appears to be necessary for a mentoring system to be developed to test believers before they are released into the ministry, especially as related to the charismata. Apostolic/missional networks must be in the process of mentoring its believers. Second, a vigorous pneumatology must not be curtailed by a truncated eschatology. The Azusa Street Revival was tied to eschatology. In fact, the outpouring of the Spirit in 1906 was understood by many as proof that they were living in the last days. It appears that they were off a bit. CFN's pneumatology is especially powerful in at least two areas: (1) equipping the saints for active ministry and (2) valuing the knowledge of God as revealed in Scripture and experienced in life. It must not sideline the activity of the Spirit in its midst.

Appendix

While the church might be in a post-charismatic era, the kingdom of God is not. Signs and wonders accompany the spread of the gospel into the world and culture, especially unreached people groups. Third, a dependence on the Spirit is paramount to the risk-taking activity of being an apostolic/missional network and movement. Each member of CFN must learn and relearn to rely upon the Spirit in order to take the gospel outside. Last of all, Acts 1:8 must remain the center of its methodology. As new apostles, prophets, evangelists, and pastor/teachers are raised up, the proof of their effectiveness will be the lasting fruit that they produce. The future of the church will not be measured by conferences or megachurches, but by the impact it has on reaching people who are unwilling to engage Christianity within its buildings. God's kingdom will come in the world, but not necessarily inside the church facility.

Church Foundational Network is at the end of its beginning. The honeymoon is over. Its future is at hand. It's time to raise its kids, take out the trash, and budget for the family—or whatever the apostolic network equivalent is for these.

Bibliography

Ahrend, Todd. *In This Generation: Looking to the Past to Reach the Present.* Colorado Springs: Dawson Media, 2010.
Allen, Roland. *The Spontaneous Expansion of the Church and the Causes Which Hinder It.* American ed. Grand Rapids: Eerdmans, 1962.
Altizer, Thomas J. J. *The Gospel of Christian Atheism.* Philadelphia: Westminster, 1966.
Archer, Kenneth J. *A Pentecostal Hermeneutic for the Twenty-First Century: Spirit, Scripture, and Community.* Journal of Pentecostal Theology Supplement Series 28. New York: T. &. T Clark, 2004.
Arrington, French. *Maintaining the Foundations: A Study of 1 Timothy.* Grand Rapids: Baker, 1982.
Assembly of God General Council. *Apostles and Prophets: A Position Paper.* August 6, 2001. Online: http://www.ag.org/top/Beliefs/Position_Papers/pp_downloads/pp_4195_apostles_prophets.pdf.
———. *Minutes of the 50th Session of the General Council of the Assemblies of God.* Convened in Washington, DC, July 31–August 3, 2003. Online: http://ifphc.org/DigitalPublications/USA/Assemblies%20of%20God%20USA/Minutes%20General%20Council/Unregistered/2003/FPHC/2003.pdf.
Barth, Markus. *Ephesians: Translation and Commentary on Chapter 4–6.* Anchor Bible 34a. New York: Doubleday, 1974.
Barrett, David B., editor. *World Christian Encyclopedia: A Comparative Study of Churches and Religions in the Modern World.* New York: Oxford University Press, 1982.
Barrett, David B., Todd M. Johnson, and Peter F. Crossings. "Missiometrics 2005: A Global Survey of World Mission." *International Bulletin of Missionary Research* 29 (January 2005) 29.
Barrs, Jerram. *Shepherds and Sheep: A Biblical View of Leading and Following.* Downers Grove, IL: InterVarsity, 1983.
Basham, Don. "Leadership, a Biblical Look." *New Wine Magazine* 7/6 (March 1974) 14–17.
Baxter, Robert. *Narrative of Facts, Characterizing the Supernatural Manifestations in Members of Mr. Irving's Congregation and Other Individuals, in England and Scotland, and Formerly in the Writer Himself.* London: Nisbet, 1833.
Baxter, W. J. Ern. *Thy Kingdom Come.* Ft. Lauderdale, FL: Christian Growth Ministries, 1977.

Bibliography

Beckham, William A. *The Second Reformation: Reshaping the Church for the 21st Century.* Houston: TOUCH, 1995.

Berger, Peter L. *The Sacred Canopy: Elements of a Sociological Theory of Religion.* New York: Anchor, 1967.

Blessitt, Arthur, with Walter Wagner. *Turned on to Jesus.* New York: Hawthorn, 1971.

Bosch, David J. *Transforming Mission: Paradigm Shifts in Theology of Mission.* Maryknoll, NY: Orbis, 1991.

Brafman, Ori, and Rod A. Beckstrom. *The Starfish and the Spider: The Unstoppable Power of Leaderless Organizations.* New York: Penguin, 2007.

Brown, John S., and Paul Dugud. *The Social Life of Information.* Boston: Harvard Business School Press, 2000.

Bruce, F. F. *The Canon of Scripture.* Downers Grove, IL: InterVarsity, 1988.

Buckingham, Jamie. "The End of the Discipleship Era." *Ministries Today* 8/1 (January–February 1990) 46–52.

Buddy, D. D. "Edward Irving." In *The New International Dictionary of Pentecostal and Charismatic Movements*, rev. ed., edited by Stanley M. Burgess, 803–4. Grand Rapids: Zondervan, 2002.

Cada, L., G. Foley, R. Fritz, and T. Giardino. *Shaping the Coming Age of Religious Life.* New York: Seabury, 1979.

Calvin, John. *Institutes of the Christian Religion.* Edited by John T. McMeill, translated by Ford L. Battles. 2 vols. Philadelphia: Westminster, 1960.

Camp, Lee C. *Mere Discipleship: Radical Christianity in a Rebellious World.* Grand Rapids: Brazos, 2003.

Campbell, Joseph E. *The Pentecostal Holiness Church, 1898–1948.* Franklin Springs, GA: Publishing House of the Pentecostal Holiness Church, 1951.

Campbell, R. Alastair. *The Elders: Seniority within Earliest Christianity.* Edinburgh: T. & T. Clark, 1994.

Cannistraci, David. *Apostles and the Emerging Apostolic Movement.* Ventura, CA: Renew, 1996.

———. *The Gift of Apostle.* Ventura, CA: Regal, 1996.

Carlyle, Thomas. *Reminiscences.* Edited by James A. Froude. New York: Scribner, 1881.

Cartledge, David. *The Apostolic Revolution: The Restoration of Apostles and Prophets in the Assemblies of God in Australia.* Chester Hill, NSW, Australia: Paraclete Institute, 2000.

Church Foundational Network. "Articles of Incorporation." 1995. Online: http://www.cfnonline.org/downloads/cfn_charter.pdf.

Clapp, Rodney. *A Peculiar People: The Church as Culture in a Post-Christian Society.* Downers Grove, IL: InterVarsity, 1996.

Click, Bill. "The Fully Foundational Church: Combining & Mobilizing the Parts of Christ's Completeness." Part 5. Online: http://www.identitynetwork.net/Articles-?blogid=2093&view=post&articleid=50477&fldKeywords=fully%20foundational&fldAuthor=&fldTopic=0.

Cobble, James F., Jr. *The Church and the Powers: A Theology of Church Structure.* Peabody, MA: Hendrickson, 1988.

Cole, Henry. *A Letter to the Rev. Edward Irving, Minister of the Caledonian Chapel, Compton Street, in Refutation of the Awful Doctrines (held by him) of the Sinfulness, Mortality, and Corruptibility of the Body of Jesus Christ.* London: J. Eedes, 1827.

Bibliography

Cole, Neil. *Church 3.0: Upgrades for the Future of the Church*. San Francisco: Jossey-Bass, 2009.

Coleridge, Samuel T. *The Collected Works of S. T. Coleridge*. Edited by Kathleen Coburn. Princeton, NJ: Princeton University Press, 1976.

———. *On the Constitution of the Church and State According to the Idea of Each with Aids toward a Right Judgement on the Late Catholic Bill*. London. Hurst, Chance, 1830.

Collins, Jim. *Good to Great: Why Some Companies Make the Leap, and Others Don't*. New York: HarperBusiness, 2001.

Collins, Tara L., and Rebecca L. Caroline. "Senior Moments." *Liberty Church: An Oasis of Love and Hope* 12/10 (October 2011) 1.

Constitution and General Rules of the Fire-Baptized Holiness Church. Royston, GA: Live Coals Press, 1905. Online: http://pctii.org/arc/1905_bk.html.

Crumpler, A. B. *The Discipline of the Holiness Church*. Goldsboro, NC: Nash Brothers, Book and Job Printers, 1902. Online: http://pctii.org/arc/1902_bk.html.

Cox, Harvey. *Fire from Heaven: The Rise of Pentecostal Spirituality and the Reshaping of Religion in the Twenty-First Century*. Reading, MA: Addison-Wesley, 1995.

Dallimore, Arnold. *Forerunner of the Charismatic Movement: The Life of Edward Irving*. Chicago: Moody Bible Institute, 1983.

Damazio, Frank. *The Making of a Leader*. Portland: Bible Temple, 1988.

Davenport, Rowland A. *Albury Apostles: The Story of the Body Known as Catholic Apostolic Church (Sometimes Called 'The Irvingites')*. Glasgow, Scotland: United Writers, 1970.

Dawson, John. *Taking Our Cities for God: How to Break Spiritual Strongholds*. Lake Mary, FL: Creation House, 1989.

Dayton, Donald W. *Theological Roots of Pentecostalism*. Peabody, MA: Hendrickson, 1987.

Dowsett, Andrew. "Recovering the Five-Fold Ministry of the Local Church." PhD diss., St. John's College, n.d.

Drummond, Andrew L. *Edward Irving and His Circle*. London: James Clark, 1937.

Drummond, Henry, editor. *Dialogues on Prophecy*. London: Nisbet, 1828–1829.

Dunn, James D. G. *Baptism of the Holy Spirit: A Re-Examination of the New Testament Teaching on the Gifts of the Spirit in Relation to Pentecostalism Today*. Philadelphia: SCM, 1970.

———. *The Theology of Paul the Apostle*. Grand Rapids: Eerdmans, 1998.

———. *Unity and Diversity in the New Testament: An Inquiry into the Character of Earliest Christianity*. London: SCM, 1977.

Ellis, E. Earle. *Pauline Theology: Ministry and Society*. Grand Rapids: Eerdmans, 1989.

———. "Prophecy in the New Testament Church—and Today." In *Prophetic Vocation in the New Testament and Today*, edited by J. Panagopoulos, 46–57, Leiden: Brill, 1977.

Erickson, Millard J. *Christian Theology*. Grand Rapids: Baker, 1987.

Farrer, A. M. "The Ministry in the New Testament." In *The Apostolic Ministry: Essays on the History and Doctrine of Episcopacy*, edited by Kenneth E. Kirk, 113–82. London: Hodder and Stoughton, 1946.

Fee, Gordon D. *The First Epistle to the Corinthians*. New International Commentary on the New Testament Series. Grand Rapids: Eerdmans, 1987.

Flegg, Columba G. *"Gathered Under Apostles": A Study of the Catholic Apostolic Church*. New York: Oxford University Press, 1992.

Frere, James H. *A Combined View of the Prophecies of Daniel, Esdras, and St. John, Shewing that All the Prophetic Writings are Formed upon One Plan. Accompanied by an*

BIBLIOGRAPHY

explanatory Chart. Also a Minute Explanation of the Prophecies of Daniel; Together with Critical Remarks upon the Interpretations of Preceding Commentators, and More Particularly upon the Systems of Mr. Faber and Mr. Cunninghame. London: Hatchard, 1815.

Friesen, Dwight J. *Thy Kingdom Connected: What the Church Can Learn from Facebook, the Internet, and Other Networks*. Grand Rapids: Baker, 2009.

Frost, Michael, and Alan Hirsch. *ReJesus: A Wild Messiah for a Missional Church*. Peabody, MA: Hendrickson, 2009.

———. *The Shape of Things to Come: Innovation and Mission for the 21st-Century Church*. Peabody, MA: Hendrickson, 2003.

Full Gospel Business Men's Fellowship International. *The Acts of the Holy Spirit among the Baptists Today*. Los Angeles: FGBMFI, 1971.

———. *The Acts of the Holy Spirit among the Methodists Today*. Los Angeles: FGBMFI, 1971.

———. *The Acts of the Holy Spirit among the Presbyterians Today*. Los Angeles: FGBMFI, 1972.

Garrison, V. David. *Church Planting Movements: How God Is Redeeming a Lost World*. Midlothian, VA: WIGTake Resources, 2004.

Gee, Donald. "Are We Too 'Movement' Conscious?" *Pentecost* 2 (December 1947) 5.

———. "Tongues and Truth." *Pentecost* 25 (September 1953) 7.

———. *Wind and Flame: Incorporating the Former Book "The Pentecostal Movement" with Additional Chapters*. Croydon, England: Assemblies of God, 1967.

George, Carl F. *The Coming Church Revolution: Empowering Leaders for the Future*. New York: Revell, 1994.

———. *Preparing Your Church for the Future*. New York: Revell, 1992.

Giles, Kevin. *What on Earth Is the Church?: An Exploration in New Testament Theology*. 1995. Reprint, Eugene, OR: Wipf and Stock Publishers, 2005.

Goldingay, John. *Models for Interpretation of Scripture*. Toronto: Clements, 2004.

González, Justo L. *From the Beginnings of the Council of Chalcedon*. Vol. 1 of *A History of Christian Thought*. Nashville: Abingdon, 1970.

Gordon, T. David. "'Equipping' Ministry in Ephesians 4?" *Journal of the Evangelical Theological Society* 37/1 (March 1974) 70.

Graham, Billy. "I Thank God for You and Your Steadfastness in the Faith . . . Something Is Happening . . . a Move of the Spirit of God!" *Full Gospel Businessmen's Voice* 10/10 (October 1962) 2–7.

Gratsch, Edward J. "The Development of Ecclesiology." In *Principles of Catholic Theology*, edited by Edward J. Gratsch, 145–63. New York: Alba, 1980.

Grenz, Stanley J. *Theology for the Community of God*. Grand Rapids: Eerdmans, 2000.

Grossman, Cathy Lynn. "Protestants Lose Majority Status in U.S." *USA Today*, October 9, 2012. Online: http://usatoday30.usatoday.com/NEWS/usaedition/2012-10-09-NONEs-gain-influence-power-in-American-religious-and-political-life_ST_U.htm.

Hamon, Bill. *Apostles, Prophets, and the Coming Moves of God: God's End-Time Plans for His Church and Planet Earth*. Santa Rosa Beach, FL: Christian International, 1997.

Harris, R. Laird. "Church, Nature and Government of (Presbyterian View)." In *Encyclopedia of Christianity*, edited by Gary G. Cohen, vol. 1, 488–95. Wilmington, DE: National Foundation for Christian Education, 1968.

Hawthrone, Steve. "Perspective." *Mission Frontiers*, May–August 2009, 28.

Hebert, A. G. *The Form of the Church*. London: Faber, 1944.

Bibliography

Hippolytus. "The Same Hippolytus on the Seventy Apostles." In *Ante-Nicene Fathers* vol. 5, edited by Alexander Roberts and James Donaldson, translated by J. H. MacMahon. Peabody, MA: Hendrickson, 2004.

Hirsch, Alan. *The Forgotten Ways: Reactivating the Missional Church.* Grand Rapids: Brazos, 2006.

Hirsch, Alan, and Tim Catchim. *The Permanent Revolution: Apostolic Imagination and Practice for the 21st-Century Church.* San Francisco: Jossey-Bass, 2012.

Hirsch, Alan, and Dave Ferguson. *On the Verge: A Journey into the Apostolic Future of the Church.* Grand Rapids: Zondervan, 2011.

Hock, Dee. *Birth of the Chaordic Age.* San Francisco: Berrett-Koehler, 1999.

Hockens, Peter. *The Challenges of the Pentecostal, Charismatic and Messianic Jewish Movements: The Tensions of the Spirit.* Burlington, VT: Ashgate, 2009.

———. "Charismatic Movement." In *The New International Dictionary of Pentecostal and Charismatic Movements*, rev. ed., edited by Stanley M. Burgess, 477–519. Grand Rapids: Zondervan, 2002.

Hodges, Melvin L. *The Indigenous Church and the Missionary.* South Pasadena, CA: William Carey Library, 1978.

Hoefer, Herbert. "New Times, New Structures: The Second Reformation and Changing Church." *Missio Apostolica* 13/1 (May 2005) 68–76.

Holmes, Nickels J. "God's Appointments." *The Altamont Witness* 1/6 (January 8, 1912) 3.

Horton, Stanley M. *The Book of Acts.* Springfield, MO: Gospel Publishing, 1981.

Hughes, Richard, editor. *The American Quest for the Primitive Church.* Chicago: University of Illinois Press, 1988.

Hunter, Harold D. "Beniah at the Apostolic Crossroads: Little Noticed Crosscurrents of B. H. Irwin, Charles Fox Parham, Frank Sandford, A. J. Tomlinson." *Cyberjournal for Pentecostal-Charismatic Research* 1 (January 1997). Online: http://pctii.org/cyberj/cyberj1/hunter.html.

Internationaler Apostlebund. *Neue Apostelgeschichte (New Acts of the Apostles).* Frankfurt am Main: Bischoff, 1985.

Irving, Edward. *Babylon and Infidelity Foredoomed of God: A Discourse on the Prophecies of Daniel and the Apocalypse.* Glasgow, Scotland: Chalmers, 1828.

———. *The Orthodox and Catholic Doctrine of Our Lord's Human Nature.* London: Baldwin and Cradock, 1830.

Iverson, Dick. "Ministers Fellowship International." In *The New Apostolic Churches*, edited by C. Peter Wagner, 171–83. Ventura, CA: Regal, 1998.

Jenkins, Philip. *The Next Christendom: The Coming of Global Christianity.* New York: Oxford University Press, 2002.

Joiner, L. A. "Back-Seater." *Ekklesia—"I Will Build My Church!,"* September 13, 2011. Online: http://www.lajoiner.blogspot.com/2011/09/back-seater-for-number-of-years-i-had.html.

———. "Community." *LA & Teresa Joiner Ministry News.* September 2012. Online: http://www.christianallianceofministries.org/contacts#newsletters.

———. "The Greatest Need." *Ekklesia—"I Will Build My Church!,"* April 25, 2011. Online: http://www.lajoiner.blogspot.com/2011/04/greatest-need-around-1990-i-was.html.

———. "Intimacy or Intimidation." *Ekklesia—"I Will Build My Church!,"* April 16, 2009. Online: http://www.lajoiner.blogspot.com/2009/04/intimacy-or-intimidation-it-is-easy-to.html.

Bibliography

———. "'Kingdom Stuff.' Part 2: Generational Leadership Transition." *Ekklesia—"I Will Build My Church!"* October 6, 2008. Online: http://www.lajoiner.blogspot.com/2008/09/kingdom-stuff-part-ii-generational.html.

———. "Trust . . . Foundation of Team." *Ekklesia—"I Will Build My Church!,"* June 16, 2009. Online: http://www.lajoiner.blogspot.com/2009/06/trust.html.

———. "Turning Leaders into Leaders." *Ekklesia—"I Will Build My Church!,"* September 16, 2009. Online: http://www.lajoiner.blogspot.com/2009/09/turning-leaders-into-leaders-jesus-said.html.

———. "When Others Interfere with the Will of God for You." *Ekklesia—"I Will Build My Church!,"* November 23, 2009. Online: http://www.lajoiner.blogspot.com/2009/11/when-others-interfere-with-will-of-god.html.

Josephus, Flavius. *The Complete Works of Flavius Josephus*. Translated by William Whiston. Grand Rapids: Kregel, 1960.

Kay, William K. *Apostolic Networks in Britain: New Ways of Being Church*. Waynesboro, GA: Paternoster, 2007.

———. *Pentecostals in Britain*. Waynesboro, GA: Paternoster, 2000.

Kelley, Dean M. *Why Conservative Churches Are Growing*. San Francisco: Harper & Row, 1977.

Kelly, J. N. D. *Early Christian Doctrines*. Rev. ed. San Francisco: Harper & Row, 1960.

King, Joseph Hillary, and Blanche L. King. *Yet Speaketh*. Franklin Springs, GA: Pub. House of the Pentecostal Holiness Church, 1949.

Lacunza, Manuel [J. J. Ben-Ezra, pseud.]. *The Coming of Messiah in Glory and Majesty*. Translated by Edward Irving. London: Seeley, 1827.

Ladd, George Elton. *A Theology of the New Testament*. Edited by Donald A. Hagner. Rev. ed. Grand Rapids: Eerdmans, 2001.

Latourette, Kenneth Scott. *A History of Christianity*. Vol. 2: *Reformation to the Present*. Rev. ed. New York: Harper & Row, 1975.

Lewis, C. S. *The Four Loves*. New York: Harcourt, Brace, 1960.

Ligon, Bill, with Robert Paul Lamb. *Discipleship: The Jesus View (An Alternative to Extremism)*. Plainfield, NJ: Logos International, 1979.

Lindbeck, George. "Confession and Community: An Israel-like View of the Church." *Christian Century* 107 (May 9, 1990) 495.

Lindblom, Johannes. *Prophecy in Ancient Israel*. Oxford: Blackwell, 1962.

Lipscomb, Buford. "Re-Invisioning CFN." Personal notes. CFN Strategy Day. Liberty Church, Pensacola, FL. September 10, 2013.

———. "The Road Ahead: Honoring Our Past; Launching Our Future." Lecture delivered at the evening session of the CFN Family Conference, Liberty Church, Pensacola, FL, June 26, 2013.

———. "The Road Ahead: Honoring Our Past; Launching Our Future." Lecture delivered at the morning session of the CFN Family Conference, Liberty Church, Pensacola, FL, June 26, 2013.

Loisy, Alfred. *The Gospel and the Church*. Translated by Christopher Home. Philadelphia: Fortress, 1976.

MacFarlane, Graham. "The Christology of Edward Irving." In *The Only Hope: Jesus: Yesterday, Today, Forever*, edited by Mark Elliott and John L. McPake, 143–52. Edinburgh: Rutherford House, 2001.

MacIntyre, Alasdair C. *After Virtue: A Study in Moral Theory*. Notre Dame, IN: University of Notre Dame Press, 1984.

Bibliography

Maier, Harry O. *The Second Setting of the Ministry as Reflected in the Writings of Hermas, Clement, and Ignatius.* Waterloo, ON: Canadian Corporation for Studies in Religion, 1991.

Martin, Roger. *The Design of Business: Why Design Thinking Is the Next Competitive Advantage.* Boston: Harvard Business School Press, 2009.

McBirnie, William S. *The Search for the Early Church.* Wheaton, IL: Tyndale, 1978.

McConnell, D. R. *A Different Gospel: A Historical and Biblical Analysis of the Modern Faith Movement.* Peabody, MA: Hendrickson, 1988.

McDonnell, Killian, editor. "Seven Documents on the Discipleship Question." In *Presence, Power, Praise: Documents on the Charismatic Renewal*, vol. 2, *Continental, National, and Regional Documents, Numbers 38 to 80, 1975–1979*, edited by Kilian McDonnell, 116–47. Collegeville, MN: Liturgical, 1980.

McGee, Gary B. *People of the Spirit: The Assemblies of God.* Springfield, MO: Gospel Publishing, 2004.

McNutt, William R. *Polity and Practice in Baptist Churches.* Philadelphia: Judson, 1935.

McQuarrie, John. *Principles of Christian Theology.* London: SCM, 1977.

Menzies, William W. "Apostolic in Doctrine." In *He Gave Apostles: Apostolic Ministry in the 21st Century*, edited by Edgar R. Lee, 26–45. Encounter: The Pentecostal Ministry Series 1. Springfield, MO: Assemblies of God Theological Seminary, 2005.

———. "Review of David Cartledge's *The Apostolic Revolution*." *Asian Journal of Pentecostal Studies* 6/2 (July 2003) 333–35.

Miller, Basil. *Bud Robinson: Miracle of Grace.* Kansas City, MO: Beacon Hill, 1947.

Miller, Donald E. *Reinventing American Protestantism: Christianity in the New Millennium.* Berkeley: University of California Press, 1997.

———. "Routinizing Charisma: The Vineyard Christian Fellowship in the Post-Wimber Era." In *Church, Identity, and Change: Theology and Denominational Structures in Unsettled Times*, edited by David A. Roozen and James R. Nieman, 141–62. Grand Rapids: Eerdmans, 2005.

Moede, Gerald F. *The Office of Bishop in Methodism: Its History and Development.* Nashville: Abingdon, 1964.

Moore, S. David. "Shepherd Movement." In *The New International Dictionary of Pentecostal and Charismatic Movements*, edited by Stanley M. Burgess, 1060–62. Grand Rapids: Zondervan, 2002.

———. "The Shepherd Movement: A Case Study in Charismatic Ecclesiology." *Pneuma* 22/2 (Fall 2000) 22.

———. *The Shepherding Movement: Controversy and Charismatic Ecclesiology.* New York: T. & T. Clark, 2003.

Morris, Leon. "Church Government." In *Baker's Dictionary of Theology*, edited by Everett F. Harrison, 126–27. Grand Rapids: Baker, 1960.

———. "Church Government." In *Evangelical Dictionary of Theology*, edited by Walter A. Elwell, 238–41. Grand Rapids: Baker, 1984.

———. "Church, Nature and Government of (Episcopalian View)." In *Encyclopedia of Christianity*, edited by Gary G. Cohen, 1:482–87. Wilmington, DE: National Foundation for Christian Education, 1968.

Moulton, James H., and George Milligan. *The Vocabulary of the Greek New Testament Illustrated from the Papyri and Other Non-Literary Sources.* Grand Rapids: Eerdmans, 1930.

Muford, Bob. "Disciple Position Paper." Unpublished paper, 1976.

Bibliography

———. *LifeChangers*, November 1975. Held at the Holy Spirit Research Center, Oral Roberts University, Tulsa, OK.

———. "The Vision of the Local Church." *New Wine Magazine* 7/7 (July–August 1975) 4–8.

Müller, Dietrich, "Apostle." In *The New International Dictionary of New Testament Theology*, edited by Colin Brown, 1:126–36. Grand Rapids: Zondervan, 1975.

Neighbor, Ralph W. *Where Do We Go from Here?: A Guide Book for Cell Group Churches*. Houston: Touch, 1990.

Niebuhr, H. Richard. *The Kingdom of God in America*. New York: Harper, 1959.

Noble, John. *First Apostle, Last Apostle*. Coblam, Surrey, England: Mike Blount, n.d.

Norton, Robert. *Memoirs of James and George MacDonald, of Port Glasgow*. London: Shaw, 1840.

———. *The Restoration of Apostles and Prophets in the Catholic Apostolic Church*. London: Bosworth & Harrison, 1861.

O'Dea, Thomas F. "Five Dilemmas in the Institutionalization of Religion." *Journal for the Scientific Study of Religion* 1/1 (October 1961) 31–32.

Oliphant, Margaret. *The Life of Edward Irving: Minister of the National Scotch Church, London: Illustrated by His Journals and Correspondence*. London: Hurst and Blackett, 1862.

Ott, Ludwig. *Fundamentals of Catholic Dogma*. Edited by James Canon Bastible, translated by Patrick Lynch. 2nd ed. St. Louis: B. Herder, 1958.

Owens, Robert R. *Speak to the Rock: The Azusa Street Revival, Its Roots and Message*. Lanham, MD: University Press of America, 1998.

Patzia, Arthur G. *Ephesians, Colossians, Philemon*. Edited by W. Wand Gasque. Good News Commentary 11. San Francisco: Harper & Row, 1984.

Pieper, Franz. *Christian Dogmatics*. Vol. 3. St. Louis: Concordia, 1953.

Pierson, Paul E. "Historical Development of the Christian Movement." Course syllabus, Fuller Theological Seminary, 1990.

Pilkington, Georga. *The Unknown Tongues Discovered to Be English, Spanish and Latin and the Reverend Edward Irving Proved Erroneous in Attributing These Utterances to the Influence of the Holy Spirit*. London: Field & Bull, 1831.

Presbyterian Church (U.S.A.) General Assembly. *Book of Order*. Part 2 of *Constitution of the Presbyterian Church (U.S.A.)*. Philadelphia: Office of the General Assembly of the United Presbyterian Church in the United States, 1967.

Prince, Derek. *Discipleship, Shepherding, Commitment*. Ft. Lauderdale, FL: Derek Prince Ministries, 1976.

———. "The Local Church: God's View vs. Man's View." *New Wine Magazine* 5/5 (May 1973) 14–18.

Riss, Richard M. *Latter Rain: The Latter Rain Movement of 1948 and the Mid-Twentieth Century Evangelical Awakening*. Mississauge, ON: Honeycomb Visual Productions, 1987.

———. "Latter Rain Movement." In *The New International Dictionary of Pentecostal and Charismatic Movement*, rev. ed., edited by Stanley M. Burgress, 830–33. Grand Rapids: Zondervan, 2002.———. *A Survey of 20th-Century Revival Movements in North America*. Peabody, MA: Hendrickson, 1988.

Robinson, Bud. *Bud Robinson's Religion, Philosophy, and Fun*. Kansas City, MO: Beacon Hill, 1942.

Bibliography

———. *My Life's Story*. 3rd ed. 1928. Reprint, Wilmore, KY: First Fruits, 2015. Online: http://place.asburyseminary.edu/firstfruitsheritagematerial/95/.

Robinson, Joseph A. *St. Paul's Epistle to the Ephesians*. 1904. Reprint, Grand Rapids: Kregel, 1979.

Roxburgh, Alan J. "Missional Leadership: Equipping God's People for Mission." In *Missional Church: A Vision for the Sending of the Church in North America*, edited by Darrell L. Guder, 183–220. Grand Rapids: Eerdmans, 1998.

———. *The Missionary Congregation, Leadership and Liminality*. Harrisburg, PA: Trinity, 1997.

Rubenstein, Robert L. *After Auschwitz: Radical Theology and Contemporary Judaism*. Indianapolis: Bobbs-Merrill, 1966.

Ruthven, Jon. *On the Cessation of the Charismata: The Protestant Polemic on Postbiblical Miracles*. Journal of Pentecostal Theology Supplement Series 3. Sheffield, England: Sheffield Academic, 1993.

Sandeen, Ernest R. *The Roots of Fundamentalism: British and American Millenarianism, 1800–1930*. Chicago: University of Chicago Press, 1970.

Schaller, Lyle E. *The New Reformation: Tomorrow Arrived Yesterday*. Nashville: Abingdon, 1995.

———. *Tattered Trust: Is There Hope for Your Denomination?* Nashville: Abingdon, 1996.

Secker, Philip J. "Ephesians 4:11–12 Reconsidered." *Logia* 5/2 (January 1996) 59–60.

Simpson, Charles. *The Challenge to Care*. Audio recording in 4 audiocassettes. Ann Arbor, MI: Servant, 1986.

———. *The Covenant and the Kingdom*. Tonbridge, Kent, England: Sovereign World, 1995.

———. "Interview: Older . . . Wiser." *Ministries Today* 8/2 (March–April 1990) 67–71.

Smith, Oswald J. *God's Plan for Leadership*. Toronto: The People's Church, 1986.

Snyder, Howard A. *Signs of the Spirit: How God Reshapes the Church*. Grand Rapids: Zondervan, 1989.

Stetzer, Ed. *Planting Missional Churches*. Nashville: Broadman & Holman, 2006.

Stewart, James H. *Importance of Special Prayer for the General Outpouring of the Holy Spirit*. London: Religious Tract Society, 1826.

Stockstill, Larry. *The Cell Church*. Ventura, CA: Regal, 1998.

Story, Robert. *Peace in Believing: A Memoir of Isabella Campbell, of Rosneath, Dumbartonshire, Scotland*. New York: J. Leavitt; Boston: Crocker & Brewster, 1830.

Strachan, C. Gordon. *The Pentecostal Theology of Edward Irving*. Peabody, MA: Hendrickson, 1988.

Strong, Augustus H. *Systematic Theology*. Westwood, NJ: Revell, 1907.

Stronstad, Roger. *The Prophethood of All Believers: A Study in Luke's Charismatic Theology*. Journal of Pentecostal Theology Supplement Series 16. Sheffield, England: Sheffield Academic, 1999.

Sumrall, Ken. *Apostolic Fathers and Their Families*. Columbus, GA: TEC, 2003.

———. *Confidence: A Key to Victorious Living*. Charlotte, NC: MorningStar, 1994.

———. *New Wine Bottles: A Handbook on Practical Church Order and Committed Relationships*. Pensacola, FL: Liberty Creative, 1976.

———. *Practical Church Government: Organized Flexibility*. Pensacola, FL: n.p., 1982.

Sumrall, Ken, with Robert Paul Lamb. *From Glory to Glory*. St. Simons Island, GA: Souls Books, 1980.

Bibliography

Synan, Vinson. "Apostolic Practice." In *He Gave Apostles: Apostolic Ministry in the 21st Century*, edited by Edgar R. Lee, 12–24. Encounter: The Pentecostal Ministry Series 1. Springfield, MO: Assembles of God Theological Seminary, 2005.

———. *The Century of the Holy Spirit: 100 Years of Pentecostal and Charismatic Renewal, 1901–2011*. Nashville, TN: T. Nelson, 2001.

———. "The Charismatic Renewal after Fifty Years." In *Spirit-Empowered Christianity in the 21st Century*, edited by Vinson Synan, 7–24. Lake Mary, FL: Charisma House, 2011.

———. *Emmanuel College: The First Fifty Years, 1919–1969*. Emmanuel College Library Series 1. Franklin Springs, GA: Emmanuel College Library, 1968.

———. "The Fire-Baptized Holiness Church." In *The New International Dictionary of Pentecostal and Charismatic Movements*, rev. ed., edited by Stanley M. Burgess, 640. Grand Rapids: Zondervan, 2001.

———. *The Holiness-Pentecostal Tradition: Charismatic Movements in the Twentieth Century*. Grand Rapids: Eerdmans, 1997.

———. "Joseph Hillery King." In *The New International Dictionary of Pentecostal and Charismatic Movements*, rev. ed., edited by Stanley M. Burgess, 822–23. Grand Rapids: Zondervan, 2001.

———. *Oldtime Power: A Centennial History of the International Pentecostal Holiness Church*. Franklin Springs, GA: LifeSprings, 1998.

———. "Theological Boundaries: The Arminian Tradition." *Pneuma* 3/2 (Fall 1981) 38–53.

———. "Who Are the Modern Apostles?" *Ministries Today* 10/2 (March–April 1992) 42–47.

Synder, Howard A. *Decoding the Church: Mapping the DNA of Christ's Body*. Grand Rapids: Baker, 2002.

Taylor, George F. *The Spirit and the Bride: A Scriptural Presentation of the Operations, Manifestation, Gifts, and Fruit of the Holy Spirit in His Relation to the Bride with Special Reference to the "Latter Rain" Revival*. Falcon, NC: Press of the Falcon, 1907.

Thorsen, Donald A. D. *The Wesleyan Quadrilateral: Scripture, Tradition, Reason, and Experience as a Model of Evangelical Theology*. Grand Rapids: Zondervan, 1990.

Toffler, Alvin. *Future Shock*. New York: Bantam, 1970.

Towns, Elmer L. "Understanding the Cycles of Church Renewal." *Ministry Advantage* 6/4 (July–August 1996) 3.

Turner, Victor. *Drama, Fields, and Metaphors: Symbolic Action in Human Society*. Ithaca, NY: Cornell University Press, 1974.

———. *Revelation and Divination in Ndembu Ritual*. Ithaca, NY: Cornell University Press, 1975.

———. *The Ritual Process: Structure and Anti-Structure*. Lewis Henry Morgan Lectures. Chicago: Aldine, 1969.

Turner, Victor, and Edith Turner. *Image and Pilgrimage in Christian Culture*. New York: Columbia University Press, 1978.

Van Buren, Paul M. *The Secular Meaning of the Gospel*. New York: MacMillan, 1963.

Wagner, C. Peter. *Apostles and Prophets: The Foundation of the Church*. Ventura, CA: Regal, 2000.

———. *Changing Church: How God Is Leading His Church into the Future*. Ventura, CA: Regal, 2004.

Bibliography

———. *Churchquake!: How the New Apostolic Reformation Is Shaking Up the Church As We Know It*. Ventura, CA: Regal, 1999.

———. "The New Apostolic Reformation." In *The New Apostolic Churches*, edited by C. Peter Wagner, 13–25. Ventura, CA: Regal, 1998.

———. "The New Apostolic Reformation: A Search for a Name." Delivered at the National Symposium on the Post-Denominational Church, Fuller Theological Seminary, Pasadena, CA, May 21–23, 1996.

———. "New Equipment for the Final Thrust." *Ministries Today* 12/1 (January–February 1994) 28.

———. "Those Amazing Post-Denominational Churches." *Ministries Today* 12/4 (July–August 1994) 48–53.

———. *Your Spiritual Gifts Can Help Your Church Grow*. Rev. ed. Ventura, CA: Regal, 1994.

Waldrop, M. Mitchell. "Dee Hock on Organization." *Fast Company*, October–November 1996, 84.

Winter, Ralph D. "The Two Structures of God's Redemptive Mission." In *Perspectives on the World Christian Movement: A Reader*, edited by Ralph D. Winter, 45–57. Rev. ed. Pasadena, CA: William Carey Library, 1992.

Woodhouse, Francis V. *The Hamburg Schism and the Apostle Woodhouse's Teaching on the Possible Call of the New Apostles*. Edited by Seraphim Newman-Norton, translated by Thomas A. Nash. Leicester, England: Albury Society, 1974.

Wuthnow, Robert. *The Restructuring of American Religion: Society and Faith since World War II*. Princeton, NJ: Princeton University Press, 1988.

Wyngaarden, Martin J. "Theocracy." In *Evangelical Dictionary of Theology*, edited by Walter A. Elwell, 1083. Grand Rapids: Baker, 1984.

www.ingramcontent.com/pod-product-compliance
Lightning Source LLC
Chambersburg PA
CBHW050811160426
43192CB00010B/1723